finishing touches

Workbook

For Student Volumes A and B

Samuela Eckstut-Didier

PHOENIX
ELT

incorporating
PRENTICE HALL MACMILLAN

New York London Toronto Sydney Tokyo Singapore

To Fanny

Published 1995 by
Phoenix ELT
Campus 400, Spring Way
Maylands Avenue, Hemel Hempstead
Hertfordshire, HP2 7EZ
A division of Prentice Hall International

Typeset by Darren Watts

Printed and bound in Great Britain by
Redwood Books, Trowbridge, Wiltshire

British Library Cataloguing in Publication Data

A catalogue record for this book is available from
the British Library

ISBN 0-13-356692-7

7 6 5 4 3
1999 98 97 96

Contents

VOLUME A

Do the right thing

Conditional sentences

1 Read the sentences. Then answer the questions with *Yes, No,* or *Maybe.*

1. If I had time next week, I would go with Camille.

   Will the speaker have time next week? _____ .

2. Ray wouldn't be late for work so often if he lived closer to the office.

   Is Ray often late for work? _____ .

3. If the police find the bank robbers, they will arrest them.

   Will the police find the bank robbers? _____ .

4. The students wouldn't be nervous about speaking English if they spoke English more often.

   Do the students speak English often? _____ .

5. Alex and Regina would get married next year if Regina weren't going to study abroad.

   Are Alex and Regina going to get married next year? _____ .

6. I'm going to go on vacation in September if I save enough money.

   Will the speaker save enough money? _____ .

7. If I make any mistakes in this exercise, I'll ask the teacher for help.

   Will the speaker make any mistakes in this exercise? _____ .

2 Rewrite the sentences with *if.*

1. People don't go to that part of the city because homeless people constantly beg for money.

   People would go to that part of the city if homeless people didn't constantly beg for money _____ .

2. There are many homeless people because they can't find jobs.

   _____

   _____ .

3. There are no jobs because the economy is bad.

   _____

   _____ .

4. It's possible the economy will improve soon, so more people will be able to find jobs.

   _____

   _____ .

5. Maybe people will donate money to help the homeless find somewhere to live.

   _____

   _____ .

6. It's possible for the government to build cheap housing. Then homeless people will stop living on the street.

   _____

   _____ .

7. The government doesn't have enough money to provide low-income housing. That's why it doesn't do anything.

   _____

   _____ .

8. The government is afraid to raise taxes, so it doesn't have enough money.

   _____

   _____ .

9. The situation may change because it's possible there will be an election soon.

   _____

   _____ .

10. The government will be able to do something about the homeless situation. Perhaps a new leader will raise taxes.

    _____

    _____ .

Even if, in case, provided that, unless

3 Complete the letter with *even if, in case, provided that,* and *unless*.

Dear Editor,

I am writing about a problem that should concern all of us _____ we
1
do not know anyone personally who is affected by the problem. What is the problem?
The problem of homelessness, especially homeless families with young children.
_____ your readers do not know what I am talking about, they
2
should just take a walk downtown a few blocks to the east of City Hall and they will
see what I'm talking about — _____ they are blind, of course. It is a
3
problem that continues to get worse, not better. Every time I walk down Third Street, I
see longer and longer lines of mothers and children waiting for a free lunch outside
one of the city's few shelters. All of us can do something to help _____
4
we want to.

Marcia Hull
Newtown

Implied conditionals

4 Underline the sentences that contain missing conditions. Then rewrite those sentences with *if*-clauses.

Dear Natalia,

<u>Boy, would you be jealous!</u> Today I was walking down the street when right
there in front of me was a $100 bill. I couldn't believe my eyes. I haven't decided
what to do with the money yet. What would you do with it? (Of course, I would
buy you something with the money, but we all know that you don't need anything.)

Unfortunately, the rest of my life isn't so great. Jim and I argue all the time. I
would break up with him, but I'm afraid of not being able to meet anyone else. I
know that's a stupid reason to stay with someone, but I bet you would do the
same, especially at my age.

As for work, you know how that is. My boss still ...

1. *Boy, would you be jealous if you were here!* _____ .

2. _____ .

3. _____ .

4. _____ .

5. _____ .

Sentences with *wish*

5 Read the text. Then write sentences about the text using *He wishes*.

I'm very lonely because my wife is dead, and I live far from my brother. I don't have anybody my own age to talk to. What's more, I have serious problems with my health. I have to spend a lot of money on medicine. Then there are my two grown children. They never do their own laundry. In fact, they don't help much around the house. My son sometimes stays out all night. My daughter is thirty-three years old, but she isn't getting married. I can't understand why she doesn't try to find a boyfriend. I think it's time for both of my children to move out of my home and find places of their own.

1. *He wishes his wife were alive* _____ .

2. _____ .

3. _____ .

4. _____ .

5. _____ .

6. _____ .

7. _____ .

8. _____ .

9. _____ .

10. _____ .

11. _____ .

Multi-word verbs

6 Complete the sentences with the correct preposition(s).

1. A: Is the birthday party a surprise?

   B: Yes, so don't show _____ late.

2. A: Is this our stop?

   B: No, we get _____ at the next stop.

3. A: Why don't you like him?

   B: He looks _____ everyone who doesn't have as much money as he does.

4. A: How did the police find out that Liz had started the fire?

   B: Her mother turned her _____ .

5. A: Why are you upset?

   B: I just found _____ that I didn't get the job.

6. A: Why are you leaving?

   B: I can't put _____ the noise any longer.

7. A: Did you go home with Cathy?

   B: No, I ended _____ getting a ride from Liz.

8. A: Why is he going to his uncle for help?

   B: He doesn't have anyone else to turn _____ .

9. A: Do you want your glasses?

   B: I don't think they'll help. The print is so small that we probably need a magnifying glass to make _____ what it says.

Vocabulary check

7 Each sentence has an underlined word or phrase. Below each sentence are four other words or phrases marked (A), (B), (C), and (D). You are to choose the <u>one</u> word or phrase that <u>best keeps the meaning</u> of the original sentence if it is substituted for the underlined word or phrase. Circle the correct answer.

1. It was <u>difficult</u> for me to find a job.
   A. award
   B. bum
   C. exorbitant
   D. tough

2. "Steve, can I <u>have</u> a quarter? I want to get a drink, but I don't have enough money."
   A. beg
   B. bum
   C. mug
   D. nod off

3. During the flight, I <u>fell asleep</u> for an hour or so because I was very tired.
   A. begged
   B. bummed
   C. mugged
   D. nodded off

4. My husband ignores people <u>asking for money</u> in the street.
   A. begging
   B. bumming
   C. mugging
   D. nodding off

5. He was arrested for <u>robbing</u> an elderly woman in the park.
   A. begging
   B. bumming
   C. mugging
   D. nodding off

6. <u>You will feel bad</u> if you lie about what happened.
   A. Your award will bother you
   B. Your conscience will bother you
   C. Your donation will bother you
   D. Your reward will bother you

7. Some people give large <u>amounts of money</u> to organizations that help the poor and the sick.
   A. awards
   B. consciences
   C. donations
   D. rewards

8. She loved the <u>prize</u> she got for winning the race.
   A. award
   B. conscience
   C. donation
   D. reward

9. If you get a loan from the bank, you will pay <u>extremely high</u> interest rates.
   A. award
   B. bum
   C. exorbitant
   D. tough

10. We will give <u>money</u> to anybody who finds our missing dog.
    A. an award
    B. a conscience
    C. a donation
    D. a reward

Structure and written expression

8 Each sentence has four underlined words or phrases. The four underlined parts of the sentence are marked (A), (B), (C), and (D). Identify the <u>one</u> underlined word or phrase that must be changed in order for the sentence to be grammatically correct. Circle the appropriate letter.

1. I <u>won't go</u> <u>to</u> the party unless they <u>will go</u>.
         A   B C   D

2. I <u>wish</u> she <u>comes</u> <u>even if</u> it <u>rains</u>.
         A   B   C   D

3. He <u>wishes</u> he <u>had</u> more time.<u> For</u> he <u>would like</u> to help you.
          A   B   C   D

4. I <u>wish</u> it <u>is</u> easier for me to learn<u>, but</u> <u>it</u> isn't.
        A   B   C D

5. <u>If I</u> <u>were</u> you, I <u>don't</u> give <u>her</u> any money.
      A   B   C   D

6. Our teacher <u>will be</u> on time for our next class <u>if</u> <u>she</u> is sick and <u>stays</u> home.
                A   B C   D

7. I'll <u>do</u> the report <u>provided that</u> you <u>pay</u> me.<u> But</u> I can't do it for two weeks.
        A   B   C   D

8. Where <u>would you go</u> <u>if</u> you <u>can</u> <u>take</u> a trip anywhere in the world?
            A   B   C D

9. <u>I'm going to take</u> my jacket <u>in case</u> it <u>will be</u> cold<u>, and you</u> should take yours, too.
           A   B   C   D

10. The Thompsons <u>didn't have</u> a place to live for a long time.<u> So</u> <u>they</u> lived in <u>a shelter</u>.
                    A   B C   D

WHAT ARE YOU AFRAID OF?

Relative clauses

1 Underline the relative clause in each sentence. Write *subject* if the relative pronoun is the subject of the relative clause. Write *object* if the relative pronoun is the object of the relative clause. Then cross out the relative pronouns that are not necessary.

1. A man ~~that~~ I know worries all the time about getting sick. _object_

2. Some people who suffer from abnormal worry and anxiety seek help from a psychiatrist. _____

3. Some of these people take medication that the psychiatrist prescribes for them. _____

4. Sometimes the medication which they take makes them stop worrying completely. _____

5. However, there are some people that the psychiatrist will not give medication to. _____

6. The psychiatrist may ask a lot of questions that will help the people understand their problem. _____

7. The questions that he or she asks may be very personal. _____

8. Some people may not want to see a psychiatrist who asks a lot of personal questions. _____

2 Choose the right phrase from the box to complete each sentence with a relative clause. Add a relative pronoun - *that, which, who,* or *whose* - where necessary.

1. The CD player ___*that/which is on sale*___ holds five disks.

2. The teacher _____ comes from Australia.

3. The bus stop _____ is across the street from the library.

4. The only vegetables _____ are peas and carrots.

5. I love the artist _____ .

6. The war has caused a lot of problems for people _____

    _____ .

7. The first blouse _____ cost
   twice as much as the second blouse.

8. I got a gift _____ .

9. The teacher told the boys _____
   to leave the classroom.

10. Politicians always make promises to people _____

    _____ .

---

a. I eat	f. you need to get off at
b. I tried on	g. is on sale
c. I wasn't expecting	h. class he is in
d. votes they want	i. live near the border
e. paintings are in that part of the museum	j. kept kicking each other

Suffix -less

3 Cross out the noun that does *not* normally go with the adjective.

1. childless: couple   grandparents   person

2. endless: conversation game   remark

3. heartless: act   remark   story

4. homeless: building   couple   situation

5. mindless: act   remark   thought

6. priceless: money   stamp   painting

7. speechless: conversation moment   winner

8. tasteless: breakfast   flowers   vegetables

9. toothless: baby   face   old woman

10. worthless: fear   money   jewelry

Adjectives ending in -ed/-ing

4 Complete the sentences with the correct word in parentheses.

1. Swimming can be _____ . (tired, tiring)

2. I don't like to watch _____ TV programs. (bored, boring)

3. I need some help because I am _____ . (confused, confusing)

4. The news was _____ . (shocked, shocking)

5. Going for a walk is _____ . (relaxed, relaxing)

6. I'm not very _____ in seeing that movie. (interested, interesting)

7. The story was so _____ that I couldn't stop laughing. (amused, amusing)

8. I was _____ when I got the bill. (amazed, amazing)

9. Wasn't that a _____ visit? (depressed, depressing)

10. I'm so _____ about the party. (excited, exciting)

Might

5 Answer the questions with short answers. Use *might*.

1. Are you going out tonight?   *I might*   .

2. Is your brother sleeping?   _____ .

3. Has the game finished yet?   _____ .

4. Are Stephanie and Jack going to come?   _____ .

5. Is your father doing the shopping?   _____ .

6. Did Eric buy his mother a present?   _____ .

7. Will Mary come?   _____ .

8. Did you eat too much?   _____ .

Could / may / might

6 Rewrite the sentences with *possible*.

1. She might be sleeping.

    It's possible she's sleeping .

2. They may have already left.

    _____ .

3. He could faint.

    _____ .

4. She could be talking on the phone.

    _____ .

5. He might not have heard you.

    _____ .

6. They couldn't have written that.

    _____ .

7. She could have stayed later, but she didn't want to.

    _____ .

8. He may not like it.

    _____ .

9. They may not have had time.

    _____ .

10. She couldn't have made such a beautiful cake.

    _____ .

May/might

7 Rewrite the sentences with *may* or *might*.

1. It's possible he's washing the clothes.

   He may/might be washing the clothes .

2. It's possible she won't have the time.

   _____ .

3. It's possible they'll get lost.

   _____ .

4. It's possible they're training for a race.

   _____ .

5. It's possible she's visiting her mother.

   _____ .

6. It's possible he's fixing the car.

   _____ .

Could/may/might

8 Rewrite the sentences with *could*, *may*, or *might*.

1. It's not possible that that was her.

   That couldn't have been her .

2. It's not possible that I left the keys in the car.

   _____ .

3. It's possible that he didn't know where to go.

   _____ .

4. It's possible that she went swimming.

   _____ .

5. It was possible for them to go abroad, but they didn't want to.

   _____ .

6. It's possible that they didn't get to the airport on time.

   _____ .

Vocabulary check

9 Each sentence has an underlined word or phrase. Below each sentence are four other words or phrases marked (A), (B), (C), and (D). You are to choose the <u>one</u> word or phrase that <u>best keeps the meaning</u> of the original sentence if it is substituted for the underlined word or phrase. Circle the correct answer.

1. It is normal to be <u>nervous</u> before an exam, but once you start working you'll feel fine.
   A. ashamed
   B. anxious
   C. compulsive
   D. repetitive

2. It's fun to be with little children, but sometimes their <u>continual</u> questions can be annoying.
   A. ashamed
   B. overwhelmed
   C. repetitive
   D. unable

3. Extreme <u>tiredness</u> is often a sign that a person is ill.
   A. avoidance
   B. exhaustion
   C. illness
   D. reputation

4. The doctor has a good <u>name</u>.
   A. avoidance
   B. exhaustion
   C. illness
   D. reputation

5. The medical situation was so bad that the doctor felt <u>helpless with</u> all the wounded people.
   A. ashamed of
   B. confident about
   C. obsessive about
   D. overwhelmed with

6. I take a shower right after I exercise because I <u>get wet</u> easily.
   A. faint
   B. scream
   C. sweat
   D. tremble

7. I wasn't just a little afraid; I was so <u>frightened</u> that I couldn't move.
   A. confident
   B. compulsive
   C. petrified
   D. repetitive

8. They are <u>uncontrollable</u> gamblers; they can't stay away from a casino or card game.
   A. anxious
   B. compulsive
   C. repetitive
   D. terrified

9. Getting married has become <u>all he thinks about</u>.
   A. an anxiety
   B. an avoidance
   C. a compulsion
   D. an obsession

10. They took her to the hospital because she <u>collapsed</u> twice in two days.
    A. fainted
    B. screamed
    C. sweated
    D. trembled

Structure and written expression

10 **Each sentence has four underlined words or phrases. The four underlined parts of the sentence are marked (A), (B), (C), and (D). Identify the <u>one</u> underlined word or phrase that must be changed in order for the sentence to be grammatically correct. Circle the appropriate letter.**

1. The stories <u>that</u> <u>I</u> heard <u>were</u> <u>frightened</u>.
         A B   C   D

2. I could <u>lose</u> the game, <u>but</u> I was lucky because the <u>guy</u> <u>I played</u> made several
           A   B   C   D

   big mistakes.

3. It is very <u>tiring</u> for him to walk<u>, so</u> he <u>could</u> be <u>walk</u> very slowly.
            A   B   C   D

4. The woman <u>that</u> <u>I</u> was <u>talking</u> said some <u>interesting</u> things.
            A B   C   D

5. Every member of the staff <u>except you</u> <u>know</u> what <u>I</u> am talking <u>about</u>.
                          A   B   C   D

6. Every boy and girl <u>wears</u> a uniform to school<u>, but</u> the students <u>that</u> are in the upper
                     A   B   C

   grades <u>doesn't</u> wear a uniform every day.
          D

7. Neither Alan <u>nor</u> Michele <u>wants</u> to help me<u>, and</u> I'm really <u>embarrassing</u> to ask
               A   B   C   D

   anyone else.

8. The printer <u>in addition to</u> the computer <u>you want</u> <u>cost</u> more than you
             A   B   C

   <u>may have saved</u>.
       D

9. They <u>might</u> not <u>have been</u> at the store <u>where</u> their brother <u>works</u> because the
         A   B   C   D

   store was closed.

10. Nobody <u>seems</u> to know <u>that</u> car <u>is</u> parked <u>in front of</u> the building.
         A   B   C   D

PEOPLE AND OTHER ANIMALS

Past progressive

1 **Complete the sentences with the correct form of the verbs in parentheses. Use the simple past or the past progressive.**

1. A: Why didn't Cecile go to the movies?

    B: She _____ (babysit).

2. A: Why didn't Peter and Jan go out for dinner?

    B: They _____ (work).

3. A: Why didn't he take another course with that professor?

    B: He _____ (not like) her.

4. A: Why didn't you hear the teacher?

    B: I _____ (talk).

5. A: Why didn't they come home earlier?

    B: The game _____ (last) a long time.

6. A: Why didn't she have any money left?

    B: She _____ (pay) a lot for the flowers.

7. A: Why didn't Rosa hear the doorbell?

    B: She _____ (sleep).

8. A: Why didn't Harry buy the Volkswagen?

    B: He _____ (decide) to buy a Toyota.

9. A: Why did it take him so long to come out and say hello?

    B: He _____ (get dressed).

10. A: Why didn't you watch the program?

    B: I _____ (eat).

2 **Complete the questions. Use the correct form of the verbs in parentheses.**

1. A: I called you last night at 8:00, but nobody was home.

    What _____ (you/do)?

    B: I was in the garage.

    A: _____ (you/fix) that old car of yours?

    B: Yep. It broke down a couple of days ago.

A: _____ (you / fix) it completely?

B: Of course. It works like a dream now.

2. A: _____ (you / see) a woman walk by the store a few minutes ago?

   B: What _____ (she / wear)?

   A: A black hat and a long, red coat.

   B: No, I don't remember seeing anyone like that.

3. A: There was a big fight at school today.

   B: Who _____ (fight)?

   A: Robert Jenkins and Eduardo Maki.

   B: What _____ (they / fight) about?

   A: Something stupid.

   B: _____ (the teacher / try) to stop them?

   A: No, she was afraid. They're big guys.

   B: Then who _____ (break up) the fight?

   A: I did.

   B: You're kidding!

4. A: My grandmother was on the phone for almost an hour this morning.

   B: Who _____ (she / talk) to? Her boyfriend?

   A: No, her sister.

   B: What _____ (they / talk) about?

   A: Who knows?

   B: _____ (you / ask) her?

   A: No, I wasn't interested.

Present perfect simple

3 Complete the news announcements with the correct form of the verbs in parentheses. Use the present perfect simple or the simple past.

1.

The Prime Minister _____ (arrive) in Washington for talks with the Americans. He _____ (arrive) this afternoon and immediately _____ (begin) his official talks. A spokesperson for the Prime Minister _____ (report) that the talks are going very well.

2.

The police report that a fire _____ (break out) in the Jackson Building on Mercer Street. Firefighters _____ (arrive) on the scene but _____ (not completely put out) the fire yet. However, the fire department _____ (begin) its investigation to find out how the fire _____ (start).

3.

There _____ (be) a five-car accident on Interstate 19 this morning. Two of the drivers _____ (die), but the police _____ (not release) their names because nobody _____ (be able to) notify their families.

Present perfect simple vs. present perfect progressive

4 Read the text. Then write sentences about Linda and Gary. Use the present perfect simple or the present perfect progressive forms of the verbs in the box.

Linda and Gary live in Arizona. They moved there in 1993. Gary wanted to move there after he retired in 1991.

At first, it was difficult for Linda to find a job like the one she had in Chicago, but she finally found one at the University of Arizona in 1993. When they moved to Arizona, Gary started looking for a part-time job; he's still looking. Two days ago he had an interview for a job that he would like to get, but he doesn't know yet if he has gotten the job. He's waiting for a phone call from the woman who interviewed him.

When Linda and Gary moved to Arizona, they wanted to buy a new car but because of some financial difficulties, they had to buy a used car. It's not perfect, but they're satisfied with it.

Both Linda and Gary are good photographers, and there are many recent photographs of the beautiful landscape of Arizona in their home. There are great pictures of the Grand Canyon.

    They have a very nice house. Gary is painting it these days because he has some free time. He started painting it last week, and he has only two rooms to finish.

    Finally, Linda and Gary have many new friends. They're very happy in Arizona.

be	be retired	have	live	look	make	paint	take	wait	work

1. _Linda and Gary have been living in Arizona since 1993_ .

2. _____ .

3. _____ .

4. _____ .

5. _____ .

6. _____ .

7. _____ .

8. _____ .

9. _____ .

10. _____ .

Vocabulary check

5 Each sentence has an underlined word or phrase. Below each sentence are four other words or phrases marked (A), (B), (C), and (D). You are to choose the <u>one</u> word or phrase that <u>best keeps the meaning</u> of the original sentence if it is substituted for the underlined word or phrase. Circle the correct answer.

1. He won't do that kind of work because he thinks it's <u>not good enough</u> for someone with his education.
    A. abusive
    B. decrepit
    C. demeaning
    D. violent

2. A strange man kept <u>looking at</u> me on the bus.
    A. abusing
    B. flapping
    C. making a fuss over
    D. staring at

3. The house is <u>in terrible condition</u>; the owners should fix it up.
   A. abusive
   B. decrepit
   C. demeaning
   D. violent

4. People who were <u>treated very badly</u> when they were children suffer their whole life.
   A. abused
   B. flapped
   C. made a fuss over
   D. stared at

5. She loves her granddaughter so much that she <u>pays too much attention to</u> her.
   A. abuses
   B. flaps
   C. floats
   D. makes a fuss over

6. The key to the manager's safe <u>was found</u> when the cleaning crew came in to clean the building.
   A. flapped
   B. floated
   C. glanced
   D. turned up

7. The soldiers <u>had to go through</u> a lot of hard training for the secret mission.
   A. were flapped
   B. were floated
   C. were stared at
   D. were subjected to

8. My mother can <u>lie</u> on her back in the sea, but she can't swim.
   A. flap
   B. float
   C. glance
   D. stare

9. I <u>looked</u> across the street for a second and saw the strangest thing.
   A. flapped
   B. floated
   C. glanced
   D. stared

10. The flag was <u>moving back and forth</u> in the wind.
    A. flapping
    B. floating
    C. glancing
    D. staring

Structure and written expression

6 Each sentence has four underlined words or phrases. The four underlined parts of the sentence are marked (A), (B), (C), and (D). Identify the <u>one</u> underlined word or phrase that must be changed in order for the sentence to be grammatically correct. Circle the appropriate letter.

1. He <u>has been talk</u> to <u>his</u> professor about something <u>that</u> is bothering <u>him</u>.
        A   B   C   D

2. If everybody <u>does</u> things the way <u>that</u> <u>they want</u>, what <u>will happen</u>?
               A   B   C   D

3. There <u>were</u> two people <u>who</u> <u>were walk</u> down the street when I <u>fell</u>.
         A   B   C   D

4. Have <u>you</u> <u>been knowing</u> <u>your</u> girlfriend <u>for</u> a long time?
         A   B   C   D

5. We <u>didn't see</u> the accident <u>which</u> happened in front of <u>our</u> house because we <u>had</u> dinner.
        A   B   C   D

6. When <u>I</u> got into a taxi <u>at the airport</u>, I <u>couldn't</u> understand <u>his</u> English.
          A   B   C   D

7. <u>If</u> the dog <u>didn't bark</u> all the time, <u>they</u> <u>wouldn't complain</u>.
    A   B   C   D

8. <u>Every</u> student and teacher had to stay outside of <u>their</u> classroom <u>while</u> the police
    A   B   C

   <u>were checking</u> the building.
       D

9. <u>Neither</u> Bob <u>nor</u> John <u>was knowing</u> <u>his</u> father.
     A   B   C   D

10. To protect animals <u>that are in danger of becoming extinct</u>, the government
                                       A

    <u>has built</u> zoos to keep <u>them</u> away from other animals and <u>people</u>.
     B   C   D

CRIME DOESN'T PAY

Past perfect

1 Read the sentences. Then answer the questions.

1. A. They went home after they finished the test.
   B. They went home after they had finished the test.

   Which happened first – went home *or* had finished the test?

   _____ .

   Are both sentences correct?

   _____ .

   If both sentences are not correct, which sentence is wrong?

   _____ .

2. A. He didn't drive for a long time. That's why he was afraid to drive.
   B. He hadn't driven for a long time. That's why he was afraid to drive.

   Which happened first – hadn't driven *or* was afraid?

   _____ .

   Are both sentences correct?

   _____ .

   If both sentences are not correct, which sentence is wrong?

   _____ .

3. A. When I arrived at the meeting, it started. I apologized for being late.
   B. When I arrived at the meeting, it had started. I apologized for being late.

   Which happened first – arrived at the meeting *or* the meeting had started?

   _____ .

   Are both sentences correct?

   _____ .

   If both sentences are not correct, which sentence is wrong?

   _____ .

4. A. When I saw her, I remembered her well – even after 20 years. We went to the same school.
   B. When I saw her, I remembered her well – even after 20 years. We had gone to the same school.

   Which happened first – remembered her *or* had gone to the same school?

   _____ .

Are both sentences correct?

_____.

If both sentences are not correct, which sentence is wrong?

_____.

5. A. Everyone escaped from the building by the time the fire engines arrived on the scene.
   B. Everyone had escaped from the building by the time the fire engines arrived on the scene.

   Which happened first – had escaped *or* arrived?

   _____.

   Are both sentences correct?

   _____.

   If both sentences are not correct, which sentence is wrong?

   _____.

6. A. John F. Kennedy was President of the United States for a little less than three years when he died.
   B. John F. Kennedy had been President of the United States for a little less than three years when he died.

   Which happened first – had been President *or* died?

   _____.

   Are both sentences correct?

   _____.

   If both sentences are not correct, which sentence is wrong?

   _____.

Past perfect simple vs. past perfect progressive

2 **Answer the questions about the kidnapping of Charles DeLourde, a rich businessman. Use the information in the box.**

destroy the car in an accident
eat only stale bread and potato chips for four days
fight
leave their fingerprints all over the victim's car
watch the DeLourde home for weeks
not call in three days
buy airplane tickets
drive 95 miles per hour
drive the same route to work for years
sit in a red Chevrolet all night long before the day of the kidnapping

1. The kidnappers knew when nobody would be at Mr. DeLourde's home. Why?

   The kidnappers _had been watching the DeLourde home for weeks_____.

2. The police found something very surprising. What?

   The kidnappers _____.

3. Mr. DeLourde was an easy target for kidnappers. Why?

   Mr. DeLourde _____.

4. One of the DeLourdes' neighbors reported something to the police. What?

   Two men _____.

5. Mrs. DeLourde was very worried. Why?

   The kidnappers _____.

6. The kidnappers left the victim's car on the road. Why?

   The kidnappers _____.

7. The kidnappers had a car crash. Why?

   One of the kidnappers _____.

8. When the police found Mr. DeLourde, he was very hungry. Why?

   Mr. DeLourde _____.

9. The police knew they could find the kidnappers at the airport. Why?

   The kidnappers _____.

10. When the police caught the kidnappers, one of them had a black eye and the other had cuts and bruises on his face. Why?

    The kidnappers _____.

Verb tense review

3 Complete the letters on the next page with the correct form of the verbs in parentheses. Use the past perfect simple, the past perfect progressive, the present perfect simple, the present perfect progressive, the simple past, or the past progressive.

Dear Leslie,

   I'm sorry I _____ (not write) in such a long time, but it
1
_____ (take) me ages to finish my thesis. It's finally over with, so
2
that's a relief.

   Since finishing my thesis, I _____ (try) to decide what to do next.
3
I _____ (think) about going abroad for a year, but I _____
4   5
(not make up) my mind yet. Actually, before starting graduate school, I
_____ (think) about going abroad. I _____ (even apply) for a
6   7
couple of jobs as an English teacher, but then I _____ (meet) Betty and
8
you know what _____ (happen).
9
   Speaking of Betty, you'll never believe who I _____ (see) the other
10
day when I _____ (go) to the library - Lucy Martinez. (You remember her,
11
don't you - Betty's old roommate?) She _____ (come) from the library.
12
She _____ (study) there for eight hours. (She must be crazy.) Anyway, I
13
_____ (not see) her in such a long time that I _____ (not
14   15
recognize) her at first. She _____ (lose) a lot of weight.
16
   Anyway, that's it for now. Hope all is well.

                                                              Joel

Dear Joel,

   Thanks for the letter. It _____ (be) such a long time since I last _____ (hear) from
17   18
you that I _____ (start) to wonder if something _____ (happen) to you.
19   20
   Congratulations on finishing your thesis. You must be glad it's over. On the other hand, when you
see how hard it is to find a job these days, you may wish you _____ (be) still in school. Let's
21
see ... how long _____ (I / look) for a job? Six months, and I still _____ (not find)
22   23
anything decent. Things are so bad that for the past month or so I _____ (work) in a restaurant
24
as a part-time cook – if you can believe that. Well, I guess there's always hope. Debbie Ong
_____ (call) me the other day. The good news is that she _____ (get) a good job.
25   26
The bad news is that she _____ (look) for nearly a year before she _____ (find) it.
27   28
   Can't think of much else. Will write again soon.

                                                              Leslie

Conditional sentences

4 Read the sentences. Then answer the questions.

1. If my mother hadn't been sick, she would have come.

   a) What time is referred to in the *if*-clause – past, present, or future? _____ .

   b) What time is referred to in the main clause – past, present, or future? _____ .

   c) Was the speaker's mother sick? _____ .

   d) Did the speaker's mother come? _____ .

2. If he'd given us good directions, we'd know where to go.

   a) What time is referred to in the *if*-clause – past, present, or future? _____ .

   b) What time is referred to in the main clause – past, present, or future? _____ .

   c) Did he give good directions? _____ .

   d) Do they know where to go? _____ .

3. She wouldn't be so happy if her boyfriend weren't with her.

   a) What time is referred to in the *if*-clause – past, present, or future? _____ .

   b) What time is referred to in the main clause – past, present, or future? _____ .

   c) Is she happy? _____ .

   d) Is her boyfriend with her? _____ .

4. We wouldn't be so hungry if we'd brought some food with us.

   a) What time is referred to in the *if*-clause – past, present, or future? _____ .

   b) What time is referred to in the main clause – past, present, or future? _____ .

   c) Are they hungry? _____ .

   d) Did they bring some food with them? _____ .

5. The animal would have attacked them if they hadn't killed it.

   a) What time is referred to in the *if*-clause – past, present, or future? _____ .

   b) What time is referred to in the main clause – past, present, or future? _____ .

   c) Did the animal attack them? _____ .

   d) Did they kill the animal? _____ .

5 Rewrite the sentences with an *if*-clause.

1. I wasn't born in an English-speaking country, so I don't speak English perfectly.

   If I had been born in an English-speaking country, I would speak English perfectly .

2. My mother married my father, so she didn't marry another man.

   _____ .

3. I'm close to my cousins because we spent a lot of time together when we were children.

   _____ .

4. We grew up in a big house, so we all had our own bedrooms.

   _____ .

5. I had to share things with my brother and sister because my parents didn't buy us a lot.

   _____ .

6. My mother didn't have to work because my father had a very good job.

   _____ .

7. My brother didn't like school, so he dropped out and joined the army.

   _____ .

8. My sister moved far away a few years ago, so we don't see her often.

   _____ .

Inverted conditional sentences

6 Rewrite the sentences in Exercise 5 without *if*.

1. *Had I been born in an English-speaking country, I would speak English perfectly* .

2. _____ .

3. _____ .

4. _____ .

5. _____ .

6. _____ .

7. _____ .

8. _____ .

Conditional sentences

**7 Complete the sentences with the correct form of the verbs in parentheses.
(Note: Be careful! There are different types of conditional sentences in this exercise.)**

1. I didn't know you were coming by bus. I _____ (pick) you up if you

    _____ (tell) me.

2. Poor Shirley! She has to take her driver's test again. She _____ (have) her

    license now if she _____ (pass) her test the first time.

3. I love dogs, but if I _____ (have) a dog, it _____ (be) a lot of trouble.

4. I met my husband when I was studying Italian in Rome. Just think! I _____

    (never meet) him if I _____ (not decide) to learn Italian.

5. You've missed four classes in the first three weeks of the semester. If you _____

    (miss) any more, you _____ (have to) see the head of the department.

6. If I _____ (have) a baby when I was 18, he or she _____ (be)

    20 years old now.

7. I can't believe I paid so much for a cake. I _____ (not buy) it if I

    _____ (know) it was going to be so expensive.

8. Look at Howie! He has to do all that work by himself. I _____ (help) him if I

    _____ (know) how.

9. Where's the bus? If it _____ (not come) soon, I _____ (be)

    late for work.

10. People _____ (spend) more time with each other if nobody

    _____ (invent) the television.

11. I _____ (come) earlier, but my alarm clock didn't go off. Sorry!

12. It's too bad I didn't know about the concert. I _____ (go).

13. I _____ (call) the store, but I'm afraid to talk on the phone in English.

    Please do it for me.

14. I _____ (send) you a card, but I didn't have your address.

15. People say that sky-diving is dangerous. Otherwise, I _____ (take) lessons.

Vocabulary check

8 Each sentence has an underlined word or phrase. Below each sentence are four other words or phrases marked (A), (B), (C), and (D). You are to choose the <u>one</u> word or phrase that <u>best keeps the meaning</u> of the original sentence if it is substituted for the underlined word or phrase. Circle the correct answer.

1. The jury <u>said the woman was</u> guilty of the crime.
    A. armed the woman
    B. found the woman
    C. made the woman
    D. saw the woman

2. The man <u>has a weapon</u> and is considered dangerous.
    A. is armed
    B. is released
    C. is slumped
    D. is suspected

3. The bank robbers received a ten-year <u>punishment</u>.
    A. convict
    B. release
    C. sentence
    D. suspect

4. The prisoner said that the police forced him to <u>say he was responsible for the crime</u>.
    A. confess
    B. determine
    C. sketch
    D. slump

5. Can you <u>draw</u> a picture of what the man looked like?
    A. confess
    B. determine
    C. sketch
    D. slump

6. The director is trying to <u>discover</u> who started the fight.
    A. confess
    B. determine
    C. sketch
    D. slump

7. They called for a doctor when they saw the driver <u>fallen</u> over the steering wheel.
    A. confessed
    B. determined
    C. sketched
    D. slumped

8. There was no sign of <u>regret</u> on their faces; they clearly did not feel bad about what they had done.
   A. convict
   B. inmate
   C. remorse
   D. suspect

9. The police <u>think the Milton brothers were</u> involved in the bank robbery.
   A. confess that the Milton brothers were
   B. sketch the Milton brothers being
   C. determine that the Milton brothers were
   D. suspect the Milton brothers of being

10. Who could have <u>been responsible for</u> the murder?
    A. committed
    B. confessed
    C. determined
    D. suspected

Structure and written expression

9 Each sentence has four underlined words or phrases. The four underlined parts of the sentence are marked (A), (B), (C), and (D). Identify the <u>one</u> underlined word or phrase that must be changed in order for the sentence to be grammatically correct. Circle the appropriate letter.

1. If she <u>hadn't passed</u> the test <u>who</u> she took in <u>June, she</u> <u>wouldn't be</u> in college now.
         A   B   C   D

2. One of the people <u>whom</u> I invited couldn't <u>come because</u> <u>he</u> <u>had been</u> busy.
                  A   B   C   D

3. <u>Had they</u> <u>listened</u> to <u>me, they</u> <u>wouldn't get</u> lost.
       A   B   C   D

4. Everybody <u>thinks</u> that she <u>may</u> <u>have taken</u> the <u>money. When</u> she quit her job.
             A   B   C   D

5. I couldn't talk to <u>her when I got</u> <u>home because</u> <u>she</u> <u>went</u> to bed and was fast asleep.
                       A   B   C   D

6. If both governments <u>tried</u> to solve their disagreements <u>peacefully, there</u> <u>might</u> not
                 A   B   C

   <u>have</u> been a war.
     D

7. <u>Once</u> you get to the center of <u>town, you</u> should look for a sign <u>that</u> <u>it</u> says
     A   B   C D

   "Top of the Town."

8. The young people <u>wouldn't have gotten</u> to know <u>each other, had</u> <u>they</u> not <u>gone</u>

A   B   C   D

   to the youth conference.

9. Everybody in the class <u>wanted</u> to go <u>home, but</u> <u>nobody</u> moved <u>until had left</u>.

A   B   C   D

10. If they <u>had known</u>, they <u>would have gone</u> to see <u>her. Because</u> they <u>hadn't seen</u>

A   B   C   D

    her in a long time.

YOU ARE WHAT YOU EAT

The passive

1 Put an X next to the sentence if it contains an unnecessary *by*-phrase.

1. She has been treated by a doctor for her injuries and released from the hospital.

2. The Statue of Liberty was given to the United States by the people of France.

3. The test papers will be corrected by the teacher and returned to the students at the next class.

4. Bill Clinton was elected President of the United States by voters in 1992.

5. People are arrested every day by the police.

6. The film *Jurassic Park* was directed by Steven Spielberg.

7. Elenore is afraid of being beaten by her husband and has gone to the police.

8. The report would be better written by you if you made it shorter.

2 Underline the passive verb(s). If the passive is not necessary, rewrite the sentence with active verb(s).

1. The doctor had to leave because he was needed at the hospital. I'll tell him you called.

   _____ .

2. Tomorrow's reading is about the ancient city of Pompeii, which was destroyed by a volcanic eruption in the year AD 79.

   _____ .

3. Ellen is at the store now. Some ice cream is being bought.

   _____ .

4. Charles was named after an uncle who was killed in the war.

   _____ .

5. If Natalie's relatives and friends had known she was in the hospital, she would have been visited.

   _____ .

6. I was afraid because the noise that was heard was so loud.

_____ .

7. The witnesses are an elderly man and woman who do not want to be identified.

_____ .

8. I'm sorry to inform you that your application for a loan has been turned down.

_____ .

9. There was a two-car accident. The white car may have been hit by the blue car.

_____ .

10. The woman was walking down the street when a bag full of money was seen; she didn't know what to do with it.

_____ .

The passive vs. the active

3 Complete the sentences with the correct form of the verbs in parentheses.

A fire _____ (break out) in a factory on the outskirts of town this
         1
morning. Part of Renotex _____ (destroy), and damage _____
                          2   **3**
(estimate) to be at around $1.2 million. Two workers in the factory
_____ (injure) and _____ (take) to a local hospital. One
      4   **5**
firefighter _____ (treat) on the scene for smoke inhalation.
                  6
     Now that the fire _____ (put out), the cause of the fire
                             7
_____ (investigate). Our reporter on the scene _____ (learn)
      8   **9**
that a former worker at the factory _____ (see) near the main building
                                          10
early in the morning. What's more, his fingerprints _____ (find) near the
                                                          11
spot where the fire began. The police _____ (find out) the man
                                             12
_____ (dismiss) from Renotex for selling secret designs to a rival
      13
company. The man's name _____ (not release), but he _____
                              14   **15**
(pick up) and, as we speak, _____ (question) by the police. The
                                  16
investigation _____ (expect) to take at least two weeks to complete.
                    17

Causative *have/get*

4 Answer the questions. Use the words in parentheses.

1. Does she dye her hair herself? (have)

   No, *she has it dyed* .

2. Should I take care of the garden myself? (have / someone)

   No, _____ .

3. Did Miriam make her dress? (have)

   No, _____ .

4. Is Paul changing the oil? (have)

   No, _____ .

5. Has Mr. Young typed the letters? (have / someone)

   No, _____ .

6. If you had been me, would you have taken the woman to the hospital? (get / the police)

   No, _____ .

7. Are they going to take pictures at the wedding? (get / a photographer)

   No, _____ .

8. Would you prepare the food if you were inviting so many people? (get / a caterer)

   No, _____ .

9. Did you shovel the snow yourself? (get)

   No, _____ .

10. Are you going to translate the report? (get)

    No, _____ .

Causative *have*

5 Put the words in the correct order to make sentences. Then complete each dialogue with the correct sentence.

a. up / someone / you / you / did / pick / to / get?
b. get / remodel / going / to / to / you / your / are / kitchen / someone?
c. to / dry-cleaned / get / this / I / jacket / have
d. I / car / looked at / times / had / three / the / have

e. cut / need / your / you / to / get / hair
f. someone / the blind woman / to / her / has / work / drive
g. to / the / to / the / deliver / air-conditioner / store / we / going / get / are
h. have / doctor / a prescription / could / give / the / had / you / you

1. A: *You could have had the doctor give you a prescription*   .

   B: I know, but I hate to take medicine.

2. A: _____ .

   B: Can't you wash it in the washing machine?

3. A: _____ .

   B: I was wondering how she gets to her office every day.

4. A: _____ .

   B: And there's still something wrong with it?

5. A: _____ .

   B: No, we're going to do it ourselves.

6. A: _____ .

   B: I know. I've already made an appointment.

7. A: _____ .

   B: No, I took a taxi.

8. A: _____ .

   B: Don't you pay extra for that?

Vocabulary check

6 **Each sentence has an underlined word or phrase. Below each sentence are four other words or phrases marked (A), (B), (C), and (D). You are to choose the <u>one</u> word or phrase that <u>best keeps the meaning</u> of the original sentence if it is substituted for the underlined word or phrase. Circle the correct answer.**

1. Why do you always <u>remove the skin from</u> apples? You remove vitamins when you do that.
   A. cultivate
   B. distinguish
   C. lick
   D. peel

2. <u>Move your tongue around</u> the ice cream cone. It's starting to melt.
   A. Cultivate
   B. Distinguish
   C. Lick
   D. Peel

3. The two governments <u>see</u> the problem differently.
   A. cultivate
   B. distinguish
   C. peel
   D. regard

4. It's impossible to <u>tell the difference</u> between the twins. They look exactly alike.
   A. cultivate
   B. distinguish
   C. lick
   D. peel

5. She loves to <u>grow plants and flowers in</u> her garden.
   A. cultivate
   B. distinguish
   C. peel
   D. regard

6. The french fries are very <u>oily</u>.
   A. chief
   B. greasy
   C. sizzling
   D. steaming

7. The soup is <u>very, very</u> hot. Don't eat it yet.
   A. chief
   B. greasy
   C. sizzling
   D. steaming

8. If you eat food when it is <u>very, very</u> hot, you may burn your mouth.
   A. chief
   B. finely
   C. greasy
   D. sizzling

9. The <u>biggest</u> problem with their diet is that they eat too much fat.
   A. chief
   B. finely
   C. greasy
   D. ingredient

10. The main <u>part</u> of this dish is rice.
    A. chief
    B. finely
    C. ingredient
    D. regard

Structure and written expression

7 Each sentence has four underlined words or phrases. The four underlined parts of the sentence are marked (A), (B), (C), and (D). Identify the <u>one</u> underlined word or phrase that must be changed in order for the sentence to be grammatically correct. Circle the appropriate letter.

1. Regarded as <u>one</u> of the world's most serious problems<u>,</u> <u>governments</u> must do
        A   B   C

   <u>something</u> about pollution.
      D

2. Hit <u>by a car</u> on the way home from school<u>,</u> <u>an ambulance took the child</u> <u>to</u> the hospital.
       A   B   C   D

3. <u>Cultivated</u> in different parts of the world<u>,</u> <u>coffee</u> <u>is regard</u> as an important source
      A   B   C   D

   of income for farmers.

4. Your name <u>is called</u>. <u>Go</u> to the information desk and see <u>if</u> there <u>is</u> a message for you.
              A   B   C   D

5. <u>Have</u> you had <u>changed the tires</u> <u>since</u> you <u>bought</u> the car?
      A   B   C   D

6. We <u>will have to get</u> someone <u>tow</u> the car if we <u>want</u> to avoid getting a ticket.
        A   B   C   D

7. It <u>was announced</u> on TV that two of the people <u>that</u> <u>injured</u> in the accident <u>have died</u>.
       A   B   C   D

8. Everyone in the class <u>has</u> <u>the teacher</u> <u>help</u> <u>them</u>.
                      A   B   C   D

9. The street where the store is <u>is being</u> <u>repaired</u><u>,</u> so we'll have to <u>be parked</u> a few
                               A   B   C   D

   blocks away.

10. The building <u>you see</u> on your left <u>was</u> <u>built</u> <u>by builders</u> with the help of the Irish
                A   B   C   D

    government.

Men and women

Gerunds

1 **Identify the gerunds in the text and write them in the blanks below. Then write** *subject*, *object of a verb*, **or** *object of a preposition*.

In spite of the large number of marriages that end in divorce, getting married is still as popular as ever. For example, take Monica Matthieu and Pablo Romero, who started going out together two years ago and who instead of living together first – like many people they know – are getting ready for their wedding this June. Making all the preparations is keeping them busy, so they have forgotten how they had both claimed to be against ever marrying when they first met. This was especially true for Monica. Being exposed to her parents' painful divorce had convinced her that marriage wasn't for her. However, now that she has met the man with whom she intends to spend the rest of her life, she is looking forward to sharing the happiness of her relationship with her closest friends and family.

1. *getting married – subject* .

2. _____ .

3. _____ .

4. _____ .

5. _____ .

6. _____ .

7. _____ .

Gerunds – object of preposition

2 **Read the dialogues. Then complete the statement about each dialogue. Use the prepositions in the box and a gerund.**

about	for	in	of	on

1. Ms. Manly: Why is your next-door neighbor in jail?
   Mr. Miller: The police say that he stole a car.

   The police arrested Ms. Manly's neighbor _for stealing a car_____ .

2. Ken: You're late.
   Ann: I know. I'm sorry.

   Ann apologized _____ .

3. Edna: Who broke the machine?
   Chris: I'm not sure.

   Chris isn't sure who is responsible _____ .

4. Freddie: Why are you leaving?
   Marge: I've been waiting for a long time and I'm tired.

   Marge is tired _____ .

5. Mr. Soy: What do you want to be when you grow up?
   Carolina: My dream is to become an astronaut.

   Carolina dreams _____ .

6. Peggy: How long are we going to stand in line?
   Stan: I don't know, but it sure is taking a long time.

   Peggy and Stan are complaining _____ .

7. Charlie: Are you going to apply for the supervisor's job?
   Linda: I think so. It looks like my chances are pretty good.

   Linda is interested _____ .

8. Steve: Great news! I got the scholarship.
   Denise: Congratulations!

   Denise congratulated Steve _____ .

9. Paul: I just talked to the bank manager. We didn't get the loan.
   Lucy: That's your fault.

   Lucy blamed Paul _____ .

10. Alicia: All of us would like to know what will be on the test.
    Mr. Morales: Make sure you learn all the verb forms.

    Students should concentrate _____ .

Gerunds – subject of sentence

3 Rewrite the sentences with gerunds.

1. It can be dangerous to walk in that part of town late at night.

   Walking in that part of town late at night can be dangerous .

2. It could have been fun to go on the picnic.

   _____ .

3. It was foolish to appoint him treasurer of the organization.

   _____ .

4. It will take us less time to go by train than it will to go by bus.

   _____ .

5. In that city, it is unusual to see beggars on the street.

   _____ .

6. It was a mistake not to study the language before we moved to the country.

   _____ .

7. It can require very long hours to run your own business.

   _____ .

8. It would be impossible to be the only female on the team.

   _____ .

9. It has been a good experience for me to be a participant in this group.

   _____ .

10. It is very important for children to feel loved.

    _____ .

Gerunds – object of verb

4 Read the dialogues. Then complete the statement about each dialogue. Use the correct form of a verb in the box and a gerund or infinitive.

avoid	decide	enjoy	intend	keep	miss	promise	quit	recall	refuse

1. Carol: Do you go skiing often?
   Claudia: Yes, I like it very much.

   Claudia _enjoys skiing_____ .

2. Enrique: Can I bum a cigarette off of you?
   Pak: Sorry. I don't smoke anymore.

   Pak _____ .

3. Ernie: How are you going to get to the picnic?
   Abby: I think I'll drive.

   Abby _____ .

4. Police officer: Did you see the suspect in front of the house?
   Witness: I don't remember.

   The witness _____ .

5. Eun Ju: Don't be late this time.
   Will: I won't. I promise.

   Will _____ .

6. Pat: Did you talk to your brother about the money?
   Ann: No. I decided to talk about anything but that.

   Ann _____ .

7. Marcel: What's the worst thing about living in a foreign country?
   Maria: I don't get to eat my mother's cooking.

   Maria _____ .

8. Shirley: Have you made up your mind about your vacation?
   Stephanie: Yes, I'm going to Brazil for two weeks.

   Stephanie _____ .

9. Mark: Are you still on a diet?
   Brian: Yeah. I'm still trying to lose weight. It's tough.

   Brian _____ .

10. Mimi: Please help me with my homework
    Mimi's brother: No.

    Mimi's brother _____ .

Used + infinitive vs. *Be used to* + gerund

5 Complete the text with the correct form of *used* + infinitive or *be used to* + gerund. Add *not* where necessary.

I _____ (work) for the telephone company, but after four years I decided
that I needed a change. That's why I took this job at Semtex Construction. I've been here
for almost two years now, and I have to admit that I really like working here more because
I _____ (make) as much at the telephone company as I'm making here.
Also, I _____ (work) with the guys in my department; I really like them. However,
at first it sure was difficult. I _____ (do) so much physical labor, and my back
_____ (kill) me at the end of every day. Then there was the problem with the
guys. I was the first woman ever to work in my division, so the men _____ (have)
a woman around. They complained that before I was hired they _____ (be able)
to talk about anything, but with me around they just didn't feel as comfortable. Now,
however, they _____ (be) around me so much that they don't even notice me
anymore. (I don't know how much I like that.) As for my back, I _____ (lift) heavy
weights now, so I am physically much stronger than I _____ (be).

Derived forms

6 Complete the sentences with the correct word in parentheses.

1. _____ is against the law. (Discriminate, Discrimination)

2. We don't want to _____ you to hire more women, but we hope you
   will. (oblige, obligation)

3. The women's organization is looking for _____ of its proposal.
   (endorse, endorsement)

4. Ms. Paterson's _____ as president of the company came as a
   surprise to everyone. (resign, resignation)

5. It is important that girls' math scores _____ boys' math scores.
   (equal, equality)

6. Teachers are looking for more _____ from fathers in their children's
   education. (involve, involvement)

7. It is your _____ to take care of the problem. (responsible, responsibility)

8. We want our female students to _____ to the same valued professions as our male students. (aspire, aspiration)

9. _____ of girls from the soccer team is not fair. (Exclude, Exclusion)

10. I don't want to _____ you, but it will be difficult for you to get the promotion. (discourage, discouragement)

Vocabulary check

7 Each sentence has an underlined word or phrase. Below each sentence are four other words or phrases marked (A), (B), (C), and (D). You are to choose the <u>one</u> word or phrase that <u>best keeps the meaning</u> of the original sentence if it is substituted for the underlined word or phrase. Circle the correct answer.

1. I <u>don't agree with</u> having to get permission from a government official.
   A. defend
   B. am devoted to
   C. exclude
   D. object to

2. There are certain colleges in the United States that <u>don't allow</u> men.
   A. defend
   B. are devoted to
   C. exclude
   D. object to

3. <u>A very, very large</u> number of people never received the information.
   A. A devoted
   B. A disastrous
   C. An overwhelming
   D. A skeptical

4. They are <u>doubtful</u> of his ability to do the job.
   A. devoted
   B. disastrous
   C. overwhelming
   D. skeptical

5. The flood was <u>extremely bad</u>; mostly everything in the area was destroyed.
   A. devoted
   B. disastrous
   C. overwhelming
   D. skeptical

6. <u>Unequal treatment</u> because of sex, race, or religion is against the law.
   A. Aspiration
   B. Discrimination
   C. Obstacle
   D. Prospect

7. Your job <u>possibilities</u> without a college education are not good.
   A. aspirations
   B. discrimination
   C. obstacles
   D. prospects

8. Some people think they need to own a gun in order to <u>protect</u> themselves.
   A. collapse
   B. defend
   C. devote
   D. exclude

9. It is common for parents to have great <u>hopes</u> for their children's future.
   A. aspirations
   B. objections
   C. obstacles
   D. prospects

10. They have <u>spent their whole lives</u> taking care of their disabled daughter.
    A. collapsed their whole lives into
    B. defended their whole lives from
    C. devoted their whole lives to
    D. excluded their whole lives from

Structure and written expression

8 Each sentence has four underlined words or phrases. The four underlined parts of the sentence are marked (A), (B), (C), and (D). Identify the <u>one</u> underlined word or phrase that must be changed in order for the sentence to be grammatically correct. Circle the appropriate letter.

1. Women <u>who</u> work outside the home still make less money than men. <u>Although</u> there
        A   B

   <u>are</u> more and more women in <u>management positions</u>.
   C   D

2. <u>While may</u> say she is in favor of <u>helping</u> me, <u>I</u> haven't <u>seen</u> her do anything yet.
      A   B   C   D

3. <u>Being expose</u> to the virus could lead to serious illness <u>though</u> <u>doctors</u> are not sure why.
    A   B   C   D

4. They went ahead with the proposal without <u>me</u> <u>knowing</u> anything; therefore, <u>I</u> accept

                                                              A   B   C

   <u>no</u> responsibility in the event that something should go wrong.

D

5. When <u>the professor</u> began <u>to speak</u> with the words, "I regret <u>informing</u> you," I knew

           A   B   C

   <u>I hadn't been accepted.</u>

        D

6. <u>While</u> they <u>are used</u> to <u>live</u> in a cold climate, <u>the</u> weather this winter has seemed

  A   B   C   D

   exceptionally cold.

7. After <u>the police</u> arrested Jack Robinson<u>. He</u> admitted to <u>having</u> <u>committed</u> the car thefts.

      A   B   C   D

8. I don't worry about <u>not having</u> made a lot of money in the past<u>. But</u> I am concerned

                       A   B   C

   about <u>being</u> unable to earn enough money to feed my family now.

     D

9. She was lucky to <u>have</u> <u>given</u> <u>everything she</u> wanted when she <u>was growing up</u>.

                A   B   C   D

10. <u>Had he been</u> upset about <u>being laughed</u> <u>at</u> at the party last Saturday, he

    A   B   C

    <u>wouldn't stay</u> until the end.

    D

VOLUME B

WHAT PRICE PROGRESS?

Defining and non-defining relative clauses

1 Complete each sentence with a relative pronoun. Use *which, who,* or *whose*.

1. Many things ___which___ are taken for granted today did not catch on when they were first created.

2. Just consider the case of the umbrella, _____ is so much a part of our daily lives today.

3. Its creator, _____ name is not generally known, was laughed off the street when he first introduced his creation to the public.

4. That's why the inventors _____ are showing their latest creations at this year's annual Unknown Inventors Conference are confident that one day their inventions will be useful.

5. That's what I heard from a woman _____ invention of an automatic table-setter caught my eye at the conference.

6. I got a full explanation of how the table-setter works from Bea Archer, _____ has spent the last three years perfecting her idea.

7. She told me that acquaintances and relatives _____ have seen her invention often say, "Gee, Bea, it's nice, but ..."

8. She is so sure that her table-setter, _____ has already cost her $20,000, will become a household item that she is about to spend another $15,000 on making her invention better-known.

9. However, she has yet to take out a patent, _____ can cost as much as $35,000.

10. As far as I'm concerned, an automatic table-setter is nice, but setting the table is not a household task _____ is terribly time-consuming or boring.

11. To all you inventors _____ are listening to me, would one of you invent a machine that does all my ironing?

Defining relative clauses

2 It is possible to change the relative pronouns and use *that* in five sentences in Exercise 1. Identify those sentences and rewrite them with a different relative pronoun.

1. _____ .

2. _____ .

3. _____ .

4. _____ .

5. _____ .

Defining and non-defining relative clauses

3 Underline the relative clauses in the letter. Add commas where necessary.

Dear Mr. Roper,

I thought I'd write you a letter – wherever you are – to let you know what has happened since the day way back in 1896 which is the year my great-grandfather was born when you showed the world your two-wheel steam motorcycle.

5 It is hard to believe that people in those days thought that you were a man who had very strange ideas because nowadays most of us can't imagine existence without our automobile which is the descendant of your steam motorcycle. It's funny that you should have had so much trouble raising the money that you needed to open a factory since Henry Ford whose name is usually associated with the automobile made a fortune. In fact, many

10 cars which are on the road today are called Fords.

Well, you may be asking, what does the automobile look like? It has four wheels instead of the two of your steam motorcycle. (However, motorcycles do exist.) Most are fueled not by steam but by gasoline which comes from petroleum and most can seat at least four people. The driver who controls the direction of his or her car by holding a steering wheel sits on the

15 left side of the car, except in some countries where the driver sits on the right.

There have been many changes because of the common use of the automobile. First of all, people spend a lot of time driving on six- or eight-lane highways which have replaced what was woodland in your day. This is a great shame, but people these days are often in a hurry, so they need to use roads which are designed to allow speed limits of up to 65 miles

20 per hour. (In other countries, drivers are permitted to drive even faster than that.) Another destroyer of parks and other green spaces is the parking lot which is necessary if drivers are to be able to get out of their cars to go to work or to do their shopping. Drivers who park in these parking lots – luckier drivers can park on the street – have to pay for their use.

I could go on describing the changes which the descendant of your steam motorcycle

25 has caused but, hopefully, this short letter gives you a fairly good idea. It is a shame that most people whom you talked to about your steam motorcycle paid so little attention to your idea. However, now you can take some pride in knowing that you were the one who started society on this revolutionary path.

Defining relative clauses

4 The relative pronoun is not necessary in three of the sentences in Exercise 3. Identify those sentences and rewrite them without the relative pronoun.

1. _____

   _____ .

2. _____

   _____ .

3. _____

   _____ .

Defining and non-defining relative clauses

5 All of the sentences need to be completed with a relative clause. Write *defining* if the sentence needs a defining relative clause. Write *non-defining* if the sentence needs a non-defining relative clause.

1. Last night I went to a concert _____   *defining*

   _____ .

2. Theater Hall _____   _____

   _____ was packed.

3. The concert starred Sid and Rich Mariani _____   _____

   _____ .

4. The radio program _____   _____

   _____ is on 88.7 FM every Monday evening at 8:00.

5. I'm sure that most, if not all, of the people _____   _____

   _____ are devoted listeners of this very funny program.

6. During the program, people call the radio station to talk to the two brothers   _____

   _____ .

7. The callers _____   _____

   _____ sometimes ask the strangest questions.

8. If you are someone _____   _____

   _____ , you should tune in next Monday at 8:00.

6 Complete the sentences in Exercise 5 by adding these phrases. Add relative pronouns and commas where necessary.

a. are two brothers with a well-known radio program

b. attended the concert

c. can be as funny as Sid and Rich

d. seats up to 5,000 people

e. was held at Theater Hall

f. has never listened to the program

g. is called *Talk of the House*

h. answer the callers' questions about how to fix things around the house

Reduced relative clauses

7 Four of the relative clauses in Exercise 3 can be reduced. Identify those relative clauses and rewrite them as reduced relative clauses.

1. *... 1896, the year my great grandfather was born, when you showed ...* .

2. _____ .

3. _____ .

4. _____ .

8 Rewrite the sentences. Change the reduced relative clauses to full relative clauses.

1. Bill Clinton, elected President of the United States in 1992, had previously been governor of the state of Arkansas.

   Bill Clinton, who was elected President of the United States in 1992, had previously

   been governor of the state of Arkansas .

2. July 4th, Independence Day, is a national holiday.

   _____ .

3. The students standing outside the classroom are there because they are late.

   _____ .

4. The movie being filmed near the waterfront is due to come out next year.

   _____ .

5. The people living in that building will have to be evacuated.

_____ .

6. Our youngest child, born in Alaska, has always wanted to move back there.

_____ .

7. Students taking the test in Bulger Hall yesterday complained that they smelled smoke even before the fire alarm went off.

_____

_____ .

8. Her latest book, published just three months ago, is already a huge success.

_____ .

9 Answer the questions. Use reduced relative clauses in your answer.

1. Do you know the man who is sitting on the right?

No, but I know the man ___*sitting on the left*_____ .

2. Is that a picture of Thomas Edison, who was the inventor of the electric light bulb?

No. It's a picture of Alexander Graham Bell, _____

_____ .

3. Does Todd like eggs that are cooked in oil?

No. He likes eggs _____ .

4. Did the children participate in the game which was played outside?

No, but they participated in the game _____ .

5. Did the electrician fix the switch that is in the kitchen?

No. He fixed the switch _____ .

6. Did the police arrest the people who were protesting in back of City Hall?

No. The police arrested the people _____

_____ .

Vocabulary check

10 **Each sentence has an underlined word or phrase. Below each sentence are four other words or phrases marked (A), (B), (C), and (D). You are to choose the <u>one</u> word or phrase that <u>best keeps the meaning</u> of the original sentence if it is substituted for the underlined word or phrase. Circle the correct answer.**

1. You have to <u>turn off</u> the motor before you take out the key.
   A. catch on
   B. figure out
   C. shut off
   D. take off

2. If you give me a few minutes, I'll <u>understand</u> how to solve the problem.
   A. catch on
   B. figure out
   C. shut off
   D. take off

3. Doing grammar exercises can be <u>long and boring</u>.
   A. frantic
   B. hassled
   C. punctual
   D. tedious

4. Employers want their workers to be <u>on time</u>.
   A. frantic
   B. hassled
   C. punctual
   D. tedious

5. Mr. and Mrs. Frazier were <u>worried and upset</u> when their daughter disappeared.
   A. frantic
   B. hassled
   C. punctual
   D. tedious

6. <u>He finally realized</u> that he didn't have enough money to buy the car.
   A. It finally dawned on him
   B. He finally caught on
   C. He finally took off
   D. It finally took him out

7. Don't <u>leave</u> without calling me first.
   A. catch on
   B. show up
   C. take off
   D. wind

8. If the clock stops, <u>turn the dial</u>.
   A. come up with it
   B. shut it off
   C. take it out
   D. wind it

9. My professor wants me to <u>have</u> a plan for my thesis by the end of the month.
   A. come up with
   B. dawn on
   C. put up
   D. shut off

10. How much do investors need to <u>provide</u>?
    A. catch on
    B. put up
    C. take out
    D. wind

Structure and written expression

11 **Each sentence has four underlined words or phrases. The four underlined parts of the sentence are marked (A), (B), (C), and (D). Identify the <u>one</u> underlined word or phrase that must be changed in order for the sentence to be grammatically correct. Circle the appropriate letter.**

1. Red kangaroos, <u>that</u> <u>are found</u> only in Australia, <u>stand</u> as tall as or taller than a
          A   B   C D

   human being.

2. <u>The White House which</u> <u>is</u> the residence of the President of the United States, <u>is visited</u>
          A   B   C   D

   by hundreds of thousands of people each year.

3. I know you think *Moms and Pops* is <u>boring , but</u> that's the show<u>, which</u> I want to see.
                             A   B   C D

4. Since the proposal that the committee <u>has made</u> is a new way of <u>looking at</u> an old
                                   A   B

   problem. <u>We</u> would like it <u>to be studied</u>.
          C   D

5. The only <u>plan popular</u> with both parties is the Summit Plan<u>, which</u> the people do not
             A   B C

   understand <u>it</u>.
          D

6. <u>Not being</u> familiar with all the computer programs <u>that</u> are used in the office <u>causes</u>
      A   B   C

   the new assistant many difficulties, <u>he</u> will need assistance.
                                           D

7. When one thinks of the beginnings of air travel. <u>The</u> Wright brothers, <u>about whom</u>
                                                            A   B

   much <u>is known</u>, <u>come</u> to mind.
             C   D

8. If the mayor, currently <u>meeting</u> with a group of citizens, has the time, <u>he</u> will discuss
                                 A   B

   the situation with the police chief, <u>been appointed</u> to head the investigation.
                                                  C   D

9. The discoverer of penicillin, Sir Alexander Fleming, <u>whom</u> I am going to speak <u>about</u>
                                                           A   B   C

   today, made his discovery in 1928.
             D

10. If there is time, the captain wants to talk to Scott Romero, <u>who his</u> appointment last week
                    A   B   C

    <u>was canceled</u>.
      D

*F*UTURE PERFECT?

ITINERARY

7:30 PM   Flight #232 departs JFK Airport

8:05 AM   Arrival in Amsterdam

9:30 AM   Arrival at hotel

Noon   Meet other volunteers for lunch

Should

1 Tracey is going on a volunteer mission abroad. First, she is flying to Amsterdam. Use the itinerary to complete the sentences with *should* and the correct form of the verbs in parentheses.

1. It's 8:00 PM. Tracey _____ (be) on the plane, and the plane _____ (take off).

2. Meals are usually served two hours after takeoff and it's 9:30 PM, so Tracey _____ (eat).

3. Now it's 7:30 in the morning Amsterdam time, so the pilot _____ (get) ready to land the plane.

4. Let's see. It's now 9:00 AM, so Tracey _____ (arrive) in Amsterdam.

5. Tracey promised to call us at around 7:00 AM our time. It's five to seven, so she

   _____ (call) us any minute now.

6. It's noon in Amsterdam, so Tracey _____ (have) a couple of hours to rest. In a few

   minutes, she _____ (have) lunch.

7. It's now 1:00 PM, so Tracey _____ (meet) the other volunteers by now.

8. Oh. She has the afternoon free, so she _____ (have) time, I hope, to write us a postcard.

Should, could, might

2 Complete the sentences with *should, could,* or *might*. Add *not* where necessary.

1. The mechanic *should* have been able to fix the problem in no time at all. He probably just wanted to make some more money by taking his time.

2. The baby _____ be walking by the time she's 14 months old.

3. I'm not sure that my watch is right. It _____ be fast.

4. If her last name is Kasparov, she _____ be Russian.

5. It's too bad you lost your bird; the door of the cage _____ have been left open.

6. I _____ have played any better. I did the best I could.

7. It's hard to say for sure until the election takes place, but the president _____ win re-election. Everyone will be surprised if he doesn't.

8. Jack _____ be waiting in the back of the building. I'll go and see if he's there.

9. Ron _____ have gotten the job. He had the right qualifications. Why doesn't he ask the director why he didn't get it?

10. My mother _____ be on her way home. I'll tell her to call you as soon as she gets in.

11. He _____ know how to do it. Why don't you ask him if he needs some help?

12. The ride _____ take too long. It doesn't usually take more than three quarters of an hour to get there.

13. Gigi _____ have put the car in the garage. She sometimes does that if she thinks it is going to snow.

14. It _____ rain. Take your umbrella with you.

15. The video cassette recorder _____ have gone on at seven o'clock. I pressed all the right buttons. What's wrong with it?

Future forms

3 Read the sentences. Then answer the questions. Write *Yes*, *No*, or *Probably*.

1. a) The meeting will be held when Luis arrives.

    Will the meeting start before Luis arrives? _____ .

    Will the meeting end before Luis arrives? _____ .

    b) The meeting will have been held by the time Luis arrives.

    Will the meeting start before Luis arrives? _____ .

    Will the meeting end before Luis arrives? _____ .

2. a) She'll become a doctor in July.

    Will she be a doctor after July? _____ .

    Will she be a doctor before July? _____ .

    b) She'll have become a doctor by July.

    Will she be a doctor after July? _____ .

    Will she be a doctor before July? _____ .

3. a) We're going to eat dinner at 8:00.

    Will they start eating at 8:00? _____ .

    Will dinner be finished at 8:00? _____ .

b) We'll have eaten dinner by 8:00.

Will they start eating at 8:00? _____ .

Will dinner be finished at 8:00? _____ .

4. a) They are playing football at 8:00 tomorrow.

Will they start playing football before 8:00? _____ .

Will they finish playing football after 8:00? _____ .

b) At 8:00 tomorrow you'll find them at the gym, where they'll be playing football.

Will they start playing football before 8:00? _____ .

Will they finish playing football after 8:00? _____ .

5. a) When we go home, it's going to snow.

Will it start snowing before they go home? _____ .

Will it stop snowing before they go home? _____ .

b) When we go home, it will be snowing.

Will it start snowing before they go home? _____ .

Will it stop snowing before they go home? _____ .

c) When we go home, it will have snowed.

Will it start snowing before they go home? _____ .

Will it stop snowing before they go home? _____ .

Future progressive

4 Complete the sentences. Use the correct form of the verbs in the box.

fix breakfast	study	talk to Tony	wait for Anna
paint the house	swim	travel to China	work

1. A: Where will you be at 10:00 tomorrow morning?

B: I'll be at the pool. I *'ll be swimming* _____ .

2. A: Will Charlotte be at home when I come by?

B: No, she'll be at the office. She _____ .

3. A: Will the boys be able to come with us tomorrow afternoon?

B: No, they'll be at the library. They _____ .

4. A: How about if I stop by tomorrow at about 5:00?

B: That won't be good. I _____ at the airport.

5. A: Will you both be home all weekend?

B: Unfortunately. We _____ . It's a terrible way to spend a weekend, isn't it?

6. A: Can the repairman come at 8:00 to fix the stove?

   B: No, I'll be in the kitchen then. I _____ .

7. A: I'll call you at 9:00.

   B: You won't get through. My husband _____ .

8. A: What are you thinking about?

   B: Tomorrow's flight, when I _____ .

Future perfect

5 Rewrite the sentences. Use the verb in parentheses. (Note: You will need to use the passive in some sentences.)

1. The sun won't be shining at 8:30. (set)

   The sun will have set by 8.30 _____ .

2. In two months, I'll have $500 in the bank. (save)

   _____ .

3. Philip won't still be home at 8:30. (leave)

   _____ .

4. The soccer game will be over by 4:00. (end)

   _____ .

5. The food will be on the table at noon. (serve)

   _____ .

6. The children will be on the bus by 7:30. (get)

   _____ .

7. The car will be ready for you to pick up by tomorrow afternoon. (fix)

   _____ .

8. There will be no trash in the cans by 10:00. (pick up)

   _____ .

9. She won't be sleeping when you call. (get up)

   _____ .

10. You can pick up the pictures tomorrow. (develop)

   _____ .

Adjectives expressing extremes

6 Complete each sentence with a word from the box.

astounding	exhausted	freezing	gorgeous	spotless
boiling	fantastic	furious	hideous	starving
disgusting	filthy	gigantic	hilarious	tiny

1. I hope dinner is ready. I'm _____ .

2. It's so _____ that I can hardly see it.

3. Turn on the air conditioner. It's _____ in here.

4. How can you eat that ice cream cone all by yourself? It's _____ .

5. Clean up your room right now. It's _____ .

6. I wish I had my heavy coat. I'm _____ .

7. If you're _____ , why don't you go to bed?

8. She probably cleans her home every day; it's always _____ .

9. He said he was _____ with me and would never talk to me again.

10. The story was _____ ; we just couldn't stop laughing.

Vocabulary check

7 Each sentence has an underlined word or phrase. Below each sentence are four other words or phrases marked (A), (B), (C), and (D). You are to choose the <u>one</u> word or phrase that <u>best keeps the meaning</u> of the original sentence if it is substituted for the underlined word or phrase. Circle the correct answer.

1. The mother <u>yelled at</u> her son in front of all the other children.
   A. distinguished
   B. scolded
   C. scurried
   D. slammed

2. The soldiers <u>ran</u> for cover when the shooting began.
   A. distinguished
   B. scolded
   C. scurried
   D. slammed

3. It is difficult to <u>separate</u> one twin from the other.
   A. blink
   B. distinguish
   C. slam
   D. swarm

4. Don't <u>bang</u> the door when you leave.
   A. blink
   B. distinguish
   C. slam
   D. swarm

5. Slow down when you see the <u>flashing</u> light.
   A. blinking
   B. slamming
   C. sprawling
   D. swarming

6. Years ago this place was a small village; now it has become a <u>very large</u> suburb.
   A. blinking
   B. slamming
   C. sprawling
   D. swarming

7. She only likes to shop in <u>wealthy</u> neighborhoods.
   A. soothing
   B. dented
   C. swarming
   D. upscale

8. The <u>relaxing</u> sounds will calm you down.
   A. soothing
   B. dented
   C. swarming
   D. upscale

9. The <u>crash</u> took place at Elm and Essex Streets.
   A. collision
   B. dent
   C. scolding
   D. swarm

10. It'll be hard to sell the car with that <u>damage</u>.
    A. collision
    B. dent
    C. scolding
    D. swarm

Structure and written expression

8 Each sentence has four underlined words or phrases. The four underlined parts of the sentence are marked (A), (B), (C), and (D). Identify the <u>one</u> underlined word or phrase that must be changed in order for the sentence to be grammatically correct. Circle the appropriate letter.

1. A number of pages from *Tom Sawyer,* that I borrowed from the library, are missing.

             A B   C D

2. If you come over at 7:00, you should find us at home because we'll have dinner.

     A   B   C   D

3. Watching TV is okay, but I hate listening to the news which is always bad.

  A   B   C   D

4. The number of unemployed people are constantly on the rise because nobody wants

              A   B   C

    to do anything that will make a difference.

       D

5. Why are you so worried about passing the test that you are taking tomorrow since

             A   B   C

    you must have no trouble passing it?

    D

6. By the time they receive the postcard that we sent this morning, we

       A   B   C

    will already arrive.

   D

7. Had you asked for my opinion, I would have told you that two hundred dollars were a

  A   B   C   D

    lot to pay.

8. You can ask John if the report is ready because he should finish writing it by now.

           A   B   C D

9. When Joan who is 70 retires next month, she will have been working at the same

    A   B   C

    company for 50 years.

     D

10. *The Sound and the Fury* is a book wrote by William Faulkner, who was a famous

   A   B   C   D

    American author from the southern part of the country.

ALL WORK AND NO PLAY
MAKE JACK A DULL BOY

Relative clauses with expressions of quantity

1 **Rewrite each sentence in two sentences without the relative clause.**

1. We spent four hours at the first match, most of which was played in light, humid rain.

   We spent four hours at the first match. Most of the match was played in light, humid rain .

2. We had hoped to change our seats, a number of which were empty.

   We had hoped to change our seats. A number of seats were empty.

3. The players, both of whom make a lot of money, did not seem to be playing their best.

   The players did not seem to be playing their best. Both of the players make a lot of money.

4. The fans, the majority of whom had paid a lot of money for their seats, were not pleased.

   The fans were not pleased. The majority of the fans had paid a lot of money for their seats.

5. Nat Tedesco, all of whose training was in Puerto Rico, seemed to be less affected by the hot, humid weather.

   All of Nat's Tedesco training was in Puerto Rico. He seemed to be less affected by the hot, humid weather.

6. During the match, my mother-in-law kept asking about the rules of the game, a few of which she couldn't understand at all.

   During the match my mother-in-law kept asking about the rules of the game. She couldn't understand at all a few of the rules.

7. The fans were also not happy with the referee, some of whose calls they thought were unfair.

   The fans were also not happy with the referee. Some of referee's calls they thought were unfair.

8. At the end of the match we bought some souvenirs, two of which were for my husband.

At the end of the match we bought some souvenirs. Two of these souvenirs were for my husband.

2 Rewrite each sentence with a relative clause by adding a sentence from the box.

> a. We talked to several of them about this problem.
> b. They were able to get most of the money from two banks.
> c. None of the people would ever want to work for someone else again.
> d. The majority of the store owners have at least ten employees.
> e. Most of the places were either too expensive or too small.
> f. We found much of the information surprising.
> g. We managed to get very few of their employees' names.
> h. Neither of their families is involved in the business.
> i. Both of them own a successful clothing store.

1. We interviewed a number of self-employed people.

We interviewed a number of self-employed people, none of whom would ever want to work

for someone else again

2. Cindy Norton and Martha Frankel spoke to us about the difficulties they faced when they first started up.

CN & MF, both of whom own a successful clothing store spoke to us about the difficulties they faced when they first started up.

3. They needed to raise a lot of money. *most of which they were able to get them from two banks.*

4. Before they found the right location for their store, they had looked at many places.

they had looked at many places most of which were either too expensive or too small

5. The women have very little time for themselves. *neither of whose familie — (h)*

The women, we talked to several of whom about this problem, have very little time for themselves

6. A lack of time for themselves is common to all these businesspeople.

_____, several of whom we talked to about this problem._____.

7. Finding the right workers is also a problem for our store owners.

_____, for our store owners, a majority of whom have at least 10 employees._____.

8. We wondered if these businesspeople's employees were treated better than the businesspeople themselves had been treated when they were working for someone else.

We wondered if these businesspeople's employees, a few of whose names we managed to get, were treated better _____.

9. Other information is included in our article, "Are you tired of it all?"

Other information is included in our article, " ", much of which we found very surprising _____.

Reduced adverb clauses of time

3 Change the reduced adverb clauses to full adverb clauses.

1. When walking to school, my brother and I had time to talk and have fun with our friends.

   When we walked to school, my brother and I had time to talk and have fun with our friends.

2. When riding to school, our kids spend most of the time listening to their Walkmans.

   When our kids ride to school, they spend most of the time listening to their Walkmans   .

3. Before sending us off to school in the morning, my mother used to make us a big breakfast.

   _____.

4. Before going to school, my children make their own breakfast.

   _____.

5. While doing my homework, I was never allowed to listen to the radio.

   _____.

6. While doing their homework, Stephen and Rachel sit in front of the television.

   _____.

7. After getting home from school, we would always find my mother's cookies and some milk on the table.

   _____

   _____ .

8. After getting out of school, our kids go to a fast-food place with their friends.

   _____ .

9. When entering our empty house at the end of the school day, my children know to lock the door right away and not let in any strangers.

   _____

   _____ .

10. When meeting us at the front door of our home at the end of the school day, my mother always greeted each of us with a big hug and kiss.

    _____

    _____ .

11. Since having children of my own, I realize how much our way of life has changed.

    _____ .

4 Rewrite each sentence with a reduced adverb clause. Use the words in parentheses.

1. Niki left the office and remembered she needed her files. (After)

   After leaving the office, Niki remembered she needed her files .

2. She went up on the elevator and started talking to a colleague about a problem. (While)

   While going up on the elevator, she started talking to a colleague about a problem.

3. She was getting her files and she saw her boss. (When)

   When getting her files she saw her boss. .

4. She talked to her boss for half an hour and knew she had more work to do at home tonight. (After)

   After talking to her boss she knew she had .

5. She got the new job and has very little free time. (Since)

   Since getting the new job, she has very little free time.

6. She went to the supermarket and went home. (Before)

   Before going home she went to the supermarket.

7. She went home and put a frozen dinner in the microwave oven. (After)

   After going home, she put a frozen dinner in the mw oven

8. She ate dinner and talked on the phone. (While)

   While eating dinner, she talked on the phone.

9. She hung up and sent a fax. (After)

   After hanging up, she sent a fax.

10. She sent a fax and answered the phone again. (While)

    While sending the fax, she answered the phone again

11. She wrote two memos; then she went to bed. (Before)

    Before going to bed, she wrote 2 memos.

12. She moved into her new home but hasn't had any time to enjoy it. (Since)

    Since moving into her new home she hasn't had any.

Modal verbs

**5 Identify the meaning of the underlined words in each sentence. In each blank
write *ability, obligation, lack of obligation, possibility, unfulfilled possibility*[1],
impossibility, expectation, unfulfilled expectation[2], or *logical deduction*.**

[1]*unfulfilled possibility*: something was possible, but it didn't happen.
[2]*unfulfilled expectation*: it was expected that something would happen, but it didn't happen.

1. I <u>can</u> swim, but I don't like to.   _ability_

2. She lived in Mexico for twenty years, so she <u>must</u> speak Spanish.   _logical deduction_

3. You <u>must</u> be in class on time.   _____

4. We <u>didn't have to</u> get tickets for the concert since it was free.   _____

5. There's nothing in the computer to show that he was here a year
   ago. He <u>must</u> have been lying.   _____

6. I <u>could have</u> voted, but I couldn't decide who to vote for.   _____

7. I have a dentist appointment, so I <u>have to</u> go. _____

8. Shh! The baby <u>might</u> be sleeping. _____

9. Jerry's still not here yet. He <u>must</u> not be coming. _____

10. I can't find my umbrella. Someone <u>might have</u> taken it by mistake. _____

11. Josie <u>couldn't have</u> driven. She doesn't know how to. _____

12. You <u>should have</u> received the package by now. It was sent over a week ago. _____

13. Nothing happens when I turn the TV on. It <u>must</u> be broken. _____

14. I'm going to make a cake from this recipe. It <u>shouldn't</u> be difficult. _____

Have to/must

6 Rewrite the underlined part of each sentence. Use the correct form of *must* or *have to*.

1. <u>It isn't necessary for us to pay</u> this bill until the end of the month.

    We don't have to pay .

2. Look at this bill. It's much too high. <u>They probably made a mistake</u>.

    They must have made .

3. What is this service charge? <u>It wasn't necessary for us to pay</u> a service charge last month.

    We didn't have to pay .

4. I can't get through to the customer service department. <u>Other customers are probably calling</u> about their bills, too.

    They must be calling .

5. That customer service department is awful. Last time I called <u>I was obliged to wait</u> twenty minutes before I could speak to a representative.

    I had to wait .

6. <u>You were probably thinking</u> that you would never get to talk to anybody.

    You must have been thinking .

7. At least this time wasn't so bad. <u>I wasn't obliged to wait</u> as long as you.

    I had't to wait .

8. <u>They probably weren't</u> as busy.

    They must not have been .

9. <u>You most likely didn't call</u> around noon, which is the busiest time.

_____ You mustn't have ~~not~~ called _____ .

10. It wasn't too difficult for the representative to find the problem. <u>I assume there were</u> other mistakes just like the one on our bill.

_____ There must have been _____ .

11. We still have a problem. <u>It's essential for us to cut down</u> on our expenses.

_____ We must ~~be cutting~~ down _____ .

12. Look! There's the mailman. <u>He is almost certainly bringing</u> us more bills.

_____ He must be bringing _____ .

Derived forms

7 Complete the sentences with the correct word in parentheses.

1. _____ of talks is scheduled for the first of the month. (Resume, Resumption)

2. The main _____ for the job is exceptional computer skills. (qualify, qualification)

3. To _____ in the race, you must be under fifteen years of age. (participate, participation)

4. Economists say that people should save more and _____ less. (consume, consumption)

5. The _____ that she was losing a lot of money made her think about her investment. (realize, realization)

6. You will receive _____ in the mail. (notify, notification)

7. I _____ that you are interested in working on the project with us. (assume, assumption)

8. That is a _____ on your part. (presume, presumption)

9. We shouldn't _____ since there's an exception to every rule. (generalize, generalization)

10. Studying chemistry requires a lot of _____ . (memorize, memorization)

Vocabulary check

8 Each sentence has an underlined word or phrase. Below each sentence are four other words or phrases marked (A), (B), (C), and (D). You are to choose the <u>one</u> word or phrase that <u>best keeps the meaning</u> of the original sentence if it is substituted for the underlined word or phrase. Circle the correct answer.

1. He has made a two-year <u>promise</u> to the company.
   A. abundance
   B. commitment
   C. deadline
   D. dilemma

2. She looked for the report <u>hurriedly and nervously</u> when she realized it wasn't in her briefcase.
   A. abundantly
   B. drastically
   C. frantically
   D. reluctantly

3. The situation was <u>much, much</u> worse after the accident.
   A. abundantly
   B. drastically
   C. frantically
   D. reluctantly

4. They agreed to come, but they <u>didn't really want to</u>.
   A. were in debt
   B. were in a dilemma
   C. longed for
   D. were reluctant

5. I have <u>a really tough decision</u> because I don't know whether to tell the police what I know about my cousin.
   A. an abundance
   B. a commitment
   C. a deadline
   D. a dilemma

6. They <u>owe money</u> and don't know how they're going to pay the money back.
   A. are in debt
   B. have a commitment
   C. long for money
   D. meet a deadline

7. The refugees <u>badly want</u> to return to their own country.
   A. make a commitment
   B. are in debt
   C. long
   D. are reluctant

8. The <u>date by which I have to apply</u> is March 31st.
   A. barrier
   B. commitment
   C. deadline
   D. dilemma

9. The country has <u>a very large amount</u> of oil but not enough to feed its people.
   A. an abundance
   B. a commitment
   C. a deadline
   D. a dilemma

10. The offer is very <u>attractive</u>, but we aren't going to take it.
    A. appealing
    B. drastic
    C. frantic
    D. reluctant

Structure and written expression

9 Each sentence has four underlined words or phrases. The four underlined parts of the sentence are marked (A), (B), (C), and (D). Identify the <u>one</u> underlined word or phrase that must be changed in order for the sentence to be grammatically correct. Circle the appropriate letter.

1. They <u>must tell</u> the students who were <u>affected</u> that nothing could be done. <u>However,</u>
       A   B   C

   nobody <u>has been told</u> yet.
            D

2. <u>Since</u> getting her degree, <u>the job market</u> has really been tough. <u>However,</u> she applies
      A   B   C

   for every job <u>that she is qualified for</u>.
                     D

3. She <u>mustn't</u> work six days a week. <u>Nevertheless,</u> she chooses to do so <u>because</u> she
        A   B   C

   thinks that <u>it</u> will help her advance in her career.
            D

4. Before <u>they</u> <u>opened</u> the factory, they <u>must have borrowed</u> a lot of money. <u>On the contrary,</u>
           A   B   C   D

   it seems that they have been able to pay it all back.

5. Before <u>he</u> taking the job <u>that he has</u> now, <u>he</u> <u>used to work</u> for his sister.
          A   B   C   D

6. The leaders <u>with whom the president met</u> discussed various subjects,
                     A   B

   <u>which several of them</u> <u>had been</u> previously discussed.
         C   D

7. Because the <u>building</u> was not safe, we <u>must have moved</u> out of the
           A   B   C

   <u>apartment we had been living in</u> for ten years.
           D

8. The report <u>didn't have to</u> <u>be sent</u> by fax. <u>On the other hand</u>, Ms. Boccara was
            A   B   C

   afraid to rely on the <u>mail which isn't always reliable</u>.
                  D

9. While <u>walking</u> down the street, I noticed <u>something made me</u> rather <u>confused</u>.
         A   B   C   D

10. Tomorrow afternoon the head of the company <u>will be meeting</u> with the dissatisfied
                                       A

    employees, <u>some of who</u> <u>have been</u> with the company for 30 years.
         B   C   D

THE WORLD WE LIVE IN

Should/ought to

1 Complete the letters with the verbs in the boxes and *should* or *ought to*. Use *ought to* in eight blanks and *should* in five blanks. Add *not* where necessary. (Note: You will need to use two verbs in the first box twice.)

PROBLEMS FOR SYLVIA

1.

cheat	do	help	let	say	tell

Dear Sylvia,

I've got a problem, and I don't know what to do. My manager is always taking advantage of a guy I work with — let's call him "Joe." Joe is a good worker but a very timid guy, and he's afraid of everyone, especially the manager. That's why, when the manager yells at him for no reason, Joe says nothing. I've told Joe he _shouldn't let_ anyone talk to him like that, but Joe always says, "What _should I do_ to stop him? Punch him in the nose?" "No," I've said, "You _ought to tell_ the manager to treat you with respect, like he treats everyone else."

Now there's a new problem. For the past three weeks, Joe's paycheck has been short of money, about $100 short each week. I think the manager is doing it on purpose since he knows Joe won't say anything. (If he is, I think it's disgusting. Nobody _ought to cheat_ anybody of their hard-earned money.) Well, Joe says plenty to me; he doesn't stop complaining about it. I've told Joe he _should say_ something about the missing money, but he says he can't and wants me to instead. I don't know; maybe I _ought to help_ Joe out. What _should I do_? _Should I say_ something to the manager on Joe's behalf?

Concerned

2.

check	encourage	get involved	get up the nerve	mind your own business

Dear Concerned,

It's admirable of you to care so much about your fellow worker, but frankly you _ought to mind your own business_ . You _shouldn't get involved_ in
                                                    9   10
Joe's problems. Joe _ought to get up the nerve_ to talk to the boss himself.
                            11
You _should encourage_ him to do so. Perhaps you could give him
        12
some ideas about what to say, but that's it. Joe needs to learn to stand up for himself. One more piece of advice: You _ought to check_ your
                                                               13
paycheck carefully every week. If the manager is cheating one person, who's to say he's not cheating others – including you?

Sylvia

Should/have to

2 Complete the sentences with the correct form of *have to* or *should*. Add *not* where necessary.

1. You _shouldn't_ come before two o'clock because nobody will be here to let you in.

2. Children _~ —— ~_ disobey their parents.

3. If you don't know what's wrong with the car, you _should_ take it to a mechanic.

4. To register for the exam, you _have to_ bring $20 and your identification card; if you don't, you won't be able to register.

5. We _should_ take Route 10 at this time of day; it's always crowded.

6. The company _does not have to_ pay any fines because it has agreed to take responsibility for the clean-up.

7. Some of the students in my class _don't have to._ learn English, but they want to.

8. For this kind of computer, you _have to_ use a special disc; the computer won't work without it.

9. You _should not_ use bleach to wash colored clothes. If you do, the clothes will lose their color.

10. Since it's always difficult to find a parking space downtown, you _should_ take the subway and leave your car at home.

Inversion of negative adverbs

3 Rewrite each sentence so that the adverbial phrase is not emphasized.

1. Not until quite recently had I given it much thought.

   I hadn't given it much thought until quite recently   .

2. Only once while I was sitting in the waiting room did I see anyone enter.

   _____ .

3. Only when people find themselves in a similar situation do they fully understand what it is like.

   _____

   _____ .

4. Only if you go will I go.

   _____ .

5. Not only did the police officers go to jail for one year, but each one also paid a $50,000 fine.

   _____ .

6. Not since 1973 has the region been hit by such bad weather conditions.

   _____ .

7. Not for one moment would I think them capable of such an awful crime.

   _____ .

8. No longer can people throw things away without thinking about the consequences.

   _____ .

4 Put the words in the correct order to make sentences with negative emphasis. Then write each sentence in the correct blank, according to where you are likely to see or hear each sentence.

a. home / ever / a / there / of / hardly / is / reminder
b. could / world / like / met / in / I / nowhere / you / the / else / someone / have
c. taxes / again / will / higher / pay / you / never
d. no / in / this / circumstances / water / should / be / under / put
e. should / leave / case / baggage / unattended / no / in / your / you
f. operate / to / it / necessary / rarely / is
g. that / want / again / do / to / never / I / you / see / do

1. An advertisement for a vacation spot:

   Hardly ever is there a reminder of home .

2. A speech before an election:

   Never again will you pay higer taxes. .

3. A sign at an airport:

   In no case should you leave your baggage unattended.

4. A warning on an electrical appliance:

   Under no circumstances should water be put ~~in the~~ in this .

5. A doctor talking to a patient:

   Rarely is it necessary to operate .

6. Someone before proposing marriage:

   Nowhere in the world ~~have~~ could I met someone like you.

7. A teacher talking to a student:

   Never again do I want to see you do that. .

Noun clauses

5 Complete the story with noun clauses.

Have I ever told you _why we moved here_ 15 years ago? We loved our other home, but we
                          1
were forced to move because of an environmental disaster in our own backyard. It all

happened one hot summer night. We had gotten home late that night. I'm not sure

_____ , but it must have been around 2:00 AM. When we got out of the car,
          2
there was a terrible smell. We wondered _____ . We had never smelled
                                                  3
anything like it before; it was awful. It was too late to find out _____ , so we
                                                                              4
decided that in the morning we would look to see if it was coming from our backyard. We

doubted _____ , but we had to be sure. At about 7:00 in the morning, we woke
              5
up to a lot of commotion. It seemed like the whole neighborhood was outside our house. One

man was talking to the crowd. We didn't know _____ ; we had never seen him
                                                        6
before. We got dressed quickly and went outside. We found out that everybody was there

because of the terrible smell. Our neighbors wondered _____ since none of
                                                                7

them could sleep all night. They were surprised that the smell hadn't kept us awake, too. After much discussion, we decided to call the police. When two officers arrived, one of them asked

_____ . I responded, "Can't you smell the problem?" The police officers
8

wandered around the area, but they couldn't figure out _____ either. They
9

thought the smell might be coming from the canal behind our house but decided to call the

local environmental agency. To make a long story short, the smell was coming from the canal. It

turned out that a local chemical company had been dumping chemicals into the canal for years.

The situation was so bad that everyone in the neighborhood had to move. We never knew

exactly _____ to clean up the canal, but we heard that it had cost something
10

like $1.6 billion.

6 **Answer the questions with a noun clause as subject of the sentence.**

1. When did dinosaurs disappear?

   _When dinosaurs disappeared_____ is not known exactly.

2. How many dinosaurs inhabited the earth?

   _____ remains a mystery.

3. How big was the dinosaur Tyrannosaurus Rex?

   _____ is amazing.

4. How often do scientists find dinosaur fossils?

   _____ is surprising.

5. Will people ever know for sure how the dinosaur died out?

   _____ is doubtful.

6. How did scientists find the first dinosaur fossils?

   _How scientists found_____ was due to luck.

7. Is it important for scientists to learn more about dinosaurs?

   _How important it is a_____ is not the point.

8. Has the Natural History Museum displayed all the dinosaur bones in its collection?

   _How the NHM has displayed._____ remains unknown.

9. Which museum has the biggest collection of dinosaur fossils?

   _____ is a matter of disagreement.

10. Why are the movies about dinosaurs so popular?

_____ is obvious.

7 Rewrite the sentences with a noun clause. Begin each sentence with a word in the box. (Note: You will need to use one of the words in the box twice.)

| How long | What | Where | Who | Why |

1. The destination of the environmental ship, *Greenworld*, is not known.

   Where the environmental ship, Greenworld, is going is not known .

2. The names of the ship's passengers are being kept a secret.

   Who the passengers of the ship's name, is being kept a secret.
   What the names of the ship's passengers are, is being kept a secret

3. The reason for this particular voyage is also not being made public.

   What ~~~~ was, is also ~~~~ .

4. The duration of the journey hasn't been decided yet.

   How long the duration of the journey is, hasn't been decided yet.

5. The environmental group's actions during their last protest upset government officials.

   Why the environmental group protested upset the government officials.

6. The location of the organization's headquarters is well-known.

   Where the location of the organization's headquarters is, is well-known.

Vocabulary check

8 Each sentence has an underlined word or phrase. Below each sentence are four other words or phrases marked (A), (B), (C), and (D). You are to choose the <u>one</u> word or phrase that <u>best keeps the meaning</u> of the original sentence if it is substituted for the underlined word or phrase. Circle the correct answer.

1. The environmentalists <u>say</u> that two local factories are responsible for the problem.

   A. claim

   B. cram

   C. tackle

   D. take up

2. We can't keep this chair here; it <u>occupies</u> too much space.
  A. claims
  B. crams
  C. tackles
  D. takes up

3. The mayor must do something to <u>take care of</u> the traffic problem.
  A. claim
  B. preserve
  C. tackle
  D. take up

4. She <u>stuffed</u> so many things into the suitcase that she couldn't close it.
  A. crammed
  B. preserved
  C. tackled
  D. took up

5. The villagers want to <u>keep</u> their traditions.
  A. claim
  B. cram
  C. preserve
  D. shrink

6. The <u>lack</u> of heating oil was a serious problem in the coldest weeks of the winter.
  A. incompatibility
  B. pressing
  C. shortage
  D. shrinking

7. Shortly after they got married, Ryan and Alison realized <u>they couldn't live together because they were very different</u>.
  A. were incompatible
  B. were pressing
  C. were respectable
  D. were shrinking

8. Keeping the atmosphere pollution-free is a <u>very serious</u> problem.
  A. incompatible
  B. pressing
  C. respectable
  D. shrinking

9. The number of young people entering medical school is <u>getting smaller</u>.
   A. claiming
   B. cramming
   C. pressing
   D. shrinking

10. It is perfectly <u>acceptable</u> to join the military rather than go to college.
    A. incompatible
    B. pressing
    C. respectable
    D. shrinking

Structure and written expression

9 Each sentence has four underlined words or phrases. The four underlined parts of the sentence are marked (A), (B), (C), and (D). Identify the <u>one</u> underlined word or phrase that must be changed in order for the sentence to be grammatically correct. Circle the appropriate letter.

1. The company <u>ought do</u> more about the <u>problem it caused</u> <u>before</u> the situation <u>gets</u> worse.
   A   B   C   D

2. We predict that our national leader <u>will do</u> little until it <u>is</u> too late. <u>Furthermore</u>, we
   A   B   C

   are going to go ahead and try <u>to solve</u> the problem on our own.
   D

3. While <u>walking</u> down the street, we noticed <u>something that</u> we <u>had never seen</u> before;
   A   B   C

   we didn't know if we <u>have to</u> call the police.
   D

4. Not only <u>do</u> <u>I expect</u> them to help, but I <u>also</u> expect them to find out
   A   B   C

   what <u>are their classmates</u> willing to do.
   D

5. Only when everyone <u>shows up</u> <u>we will be</u> able to start the meeting. <u>Therefore</u>, all of
   A   B   C

   you <u>ought to make</u> sure that you get here on time.
   D

6. <u>That</u> there are too many cars on the road <u>are</u> well-known. <u>What we need to ask</u> is
   A   B   C

   what <u>we are going</u> to do about it.
   D

7. Never again <u>we received</u> so many donations. <u>Consequently</u>, we were unable to
   A   B

   continue <u>funding</u> the program <u>that</u> we had set up after the disastrous fires.
   C   D

8. <u>Since</u> your mother's so tired, you <u>don't have to bother</u> her. <u>Moreover</u>, it would be
      A   B   C

   nice if you helped prepare dinner for <u>her</u>.
                                         D

9. Under no circumstances <u>should you</u> <u>not throw away</u> the battery <u>used in this computer</u>
                                    A   B   C

   with the rest of <u>your</u> trash.
                         D

10. You shouldn't <u>take</u> the test without <u>studying</u> for <u>it</u>. <u>Consequently</u>, you shouldn't need
                 A   B   C   D

    too much time to review the material.

SEE THE WORLD

Reporting statements and questions

1 Read the dialogue. Then complete the summary of the conversation.

"Is anybody sitting in the empty seat?" the young man asked.

"No, it's free," I replied.

"Are you from Miami?" he then asked.

"No," I explained. "I'm from Canada. I'm visiting college friends and taking a break from the cold."

"Where are you from in Canada?" he then wanted to know.

"Quebec," I replied.

"Do you speak French?"

"Yes. Do you?"

"A little," he told me. "I studied it for two years in college. How long have you been in Florida?" he then asked.

"I was in Orlando for four days and I've been in Miami since Monday."

"How long are you staying?"

"I'll be in the Miami area for another week or so."

"Well, if you're free, maybe we can meet one night for dinner or for a drink."

"I don't know," I said. "I'll have to ask my husband."

I guess that wasn't what he'd expected to hear because the conversation abruptly ended; he didn't even wait for his coffee. Before I knew it, the seat that had been empty was empty again.

I was sitting in an outdoor cafe when a young man came up to my table and asked

me if anybody was sitting in the empty seat. I replied that _____
                    1   **2**

_____ . He then asked _____ . I explained

that _____ and that _____
                    4   **5**

_____ . Then he wanted to know _____
                                                                6

I replied that _____ . Then he asked _____
                              7

_____ . I told him _____
            8   **9**

and wondered _____ . He told me that _____
                              10

_____ . He went on to tell me that _____
            11   **12**

_____ . Then he suddenly changed the topic by asking how long _____

_____ . I told him all about my trip so far saying that _____
       13

_____ since Monday. A waitress finally came over and he
       14

ordered a capuccino. Then he asked me _____ .
                                              15

I didn't see any harm in telling him that _____ .
                                                 16

When I said that, he smiled and said that if _____ .
                                                  17

I replied that _____ and explained that _____
                        18

_____ .
       19

I guess that wasn't what he'd expected to hear because the conversation abruptly ended; he

didn't even wait for his coffee. Before I knew it, the seat that had been empty was empty again.

Reporting requests and commands

2 Complete the sentences with *flight attendant* or *passenger*.

1. The _*flight attendant*_ said, "Would you please put your carry-on luggage under the seat
   in front of you?"

2. "Excuse me," the _____ said, "could you give my wife a glass of water?"

3. "Can you bring my husband a blanket?" the _____ asked.

4. "Please do not smoke until the captain turns off the 'no smoking' sign," the
   _____ told us.

5. "Would you tell us where our seats are, please?" the _____ asked.

6. "Please stay seated until the plane comes to a complete stop," the _____ told
   everyone.

7. "Could you tell me what the movie is?" the _____ asked.

8. "The captain requests that you do not use any electronic devices during takeoff and
   landing," the _____ said.

9. "Please fasten your seat belts," the _____ said.

10. The _____ said, "Could you help my wife and me fill in this customs form?"

3 Report the statements in Exercise 2 with *ask* or *tell*.

1. *The flight attendant asked me to put my carry-on luggage under the seat in front of me* .

2. _____ .

3. _____ .

4. _____

   _____ .

5. _____ .

6. _____

   _____ .

7. _____ .

8. _____

   _____ .

9. _____ .

10. _____ .

Should

4 Complete the sentences with *should* and the correct form of the verbs in parentheses. Add *not* where necessary.

1. A: I feel really bad. What I said about Carol wasn't nice. I _____ (keep) my mouth shut. I _____ (say) anything no matter what I thought. If Carol finds out, she'll be furious.

   B: Well, you _____ (call) her if you're worried.

A: And what _____ (I / say): "Oh, Carol, by the way, I said

something really nasty about you"?

B: You have a point there.

2. A: I'm so hot. I _____ (wear) a long-sleeved shirt and pants. I

_____ (wear) a t-shirt and shorts, but I didn't know it was going

to be so hot.

B: You _____ (listen) to the weather report. They said it was going to

be hot.

3. A: What _____ (we / serve) for dessert?

B: I don't think we _____ (serve) cake. Peter's on a diet.

A: Then how about fruit salad?

B: That's a good idea, but we _____ (think) about it when we were at

the supermarket. We don't have very much fruit in the house.

4. A: You _____ (eat) so much ice cream. It's fattening, you know.

B: Well, if it's so fattening, you _____ (buy) any when you did the

shopping. You _____ (come) home with some carrots instead. I

really don't understand you: one minute you tell me you have a surprise for me, and the

next minute you tell me I _____ (enjoy) it.

Modal verbs

5 Rewrite the underlined sentences with appropriate modal verbs. Use *could (have)*, *have to*, *may (have)*, *might (have)*, *must (have)*, **and** *should (have)*. **Add** *not* **where necessary.**

A: <u>It's not necessary for us to get on the plane yet.</u>

1. *We don't have to get on the plane yet* .

B: Yes, it is. Look. They're collecting tickets. <u>It's a good idea for you to take out our tickets now.</u>

2. _____

_____ .

A: The tickets aren't in my bag. Where are they?

B: <u>Perhaps they're in my bag.</u> <u>Maybe you put them there by mistake.</u>

3. _____ .

4. _____ .

A: <u>It's not possible that I put them there.</u> Oh, no! <u>I probably put them in the brown suitcase.</u>

5. _____ .

6. _____ _____ .

B: But we checked that suitcase. We can't
   get it now.

A: Well, <u>it was a mistake for you to check it.</u>   7. _____ .

   <u>It wasn't necessary for you to check it.</u>   8. _____ .

   <u>It was possible to take it on the plane</u>   9. _____ .

   <u>with us.</u>

B: It's a bit too late to tell me that now.

   <u>It was a good idea for you to tell me that</u>   10. _____

   <u>before I checked it.</u>   _____ .

A: But I did tell you. It's just that you never
   listen to me.

B: Here we go again. Let's not start that now.

   <u>It's necessary for us to explain what has</u>   11. _____ .

   <u>happened.</u>

A: What do you think <u>is a good idea for</u>   12. _____ .

   <u>us to say?</u>

B: Listen, they're calling our name on the

   loudspeaker. <u>They're probably looking</u>   13. _____ .

   <u>for us.</u> <u>All the other passengers have</u>   14. _____

   <u>probably already boarded the plane.</u>   _____ .

(Later on the plane)

B: Why are you angry with me?

A: <u>It was wrong for you to talk to me like that.</u>   15. _____ .

B: Like what? Great … this is just a great

   vacation. <u>It was a good idea for me to</u>   16. _____ .

   <u>stay home.</u>

Sentences with *wish*

6 Write *past* if the underlined verb refers to the past. Write *present* if the underlined verb refers to the present.

  1. I wish I <u>had</u> more time to study.   _____

  2. I wish I <u>hadn't let</u> him use the car.   _____

  3. Pam's parents wish she <u>had gotten</u> a scholarship.   _____

4. Ruth wishes her husband <u>hadn't lost</u> his job. _____

5. Paul wishes his teacher <u>had told</u> him what to study. _____

6. The people wish the prime minister <u>were</u> able to solve the nation's problems. _____

7. I wish you <u>had told</u> me the truth. _____

8. I wish you <u>didn't have</u> to leave. _____

9. I wish there <u>hadn't been</u> such a long line. _____

10. I wish I <u>were doing</u> something else. _____

7 Barbara's vacation was not a success. Complete the sentences.

1. Barbara went to the island of Siroco, but she hated it.

   Barbara wishes ___*she hadn't gone to Siroco*_____ .

2. The hotel room had no TV, and Barbara can't live without a TV.

   Barbara wishes _____ .

3. She took a boat to the island although there was a plane; the boat ride was very long.

   Barbara wishes _____ .

4. She paid for the hotel in advance, but she hated it.

   Barbara wishes _____ .

5. She went to the island with a cousin; she never realized her cousin was such a bore.

   Barbara wishes _____ .

6. It rained most of the time Barbara was on the island.

   Barbara wishes _____ .

7. Barbara didn't take warm enough clothing for the cool weather.

   Barbara wishes _____ .

8. Barbara's pictures didn't come out.

   Barbara wishes _____ .

9. Barbara's boyfriend didn't go with her; she was lonely without him.

   Barbara wishes _____ .

10. Nobody received the postcards she sent because she mailed them from the hotel rather than the post office.

Barbara wishes _____ .

Vocabulary check

8 Each sentence has an underlined word or phrase. Below each sentence are four other words or phrases marked (A), (B), (C), and (D). You are to choose the <u>one</u> word or phrase that <u>best keeps the meaning</u> of the original sentence if it is substituted for the underlined word or phrase. Circle the correct answer.

1. She <u>showed understanding</u> as I told her about the great difficulties my wife and I were going through.
   A. gave me her word
   B. took pity on me
   C. was elated
   D. was sympathetic

2. <u>An inner feeling</u> told me that I shouldn't trust the salesman.
   A. Elation
   B. Instinct
   C. Pity
   D. Sympathy

3. You need to <u>iron</u> that shirt.
   A. drag
   B. fold
   C. press
   D. shove

4. Her parents were <u>extremely happy</u> when she told them the good news.
   A. dragged
   B. elated
   C. instinctive
   D. sympathetic

5. When the doctor realized the child's parents had little money, he <u>felt sorry and helped</u> them and treated the sick child for free.
   A. gave his word to
   B. scrutinized
   C. shoved
   D. took pity on

6. He <u>promised</u> that he wouldn't tell anyone.
   A. dragged
   B. gave his word
   C. shoved
   D. took pity

7. He couldn't lift the chair, so he <u>pulled</u> it over to the table.
   A. dragged
   B. folded
   C. pressed
   D. scrutinized

8. The immigration officer <u>carefully examined</u> my passport before giving it back to me.
   A. dragged
   B. pressed
   C. shoved
   D. scrutinized

9. I got angry because another passenger <u>pushed</u> me as I was getting off the subway.
   A. folded
   B. pressed
   C. shoved
   D. scrutinized

10. <u>Put the top part of the paper over the bottom part</u> and it should fit in the envelope.
    A. Fold the paper
    B. Press the paper
    C. Shove the paper
    D. Scrutinize the paper

Structure and written expression

9 Each sentence has four underlined words or phrases. The four underlined parts of the sentence are marked (A), (B), (C), and (D). Identify the <u>one</u> underlined word or phrase that must be changed in order for the sentence to be grammatically correct. Circle the appropriate letter.

1. <u>Not</u> being able to <u>say no</u> when <u>people</u> need help, <u>others often take advantage of her</u>.
      A   B   C   D

2. I <u>shouldn't</u> <u>have had</u> the party at such an expensive restaurant, but <u>trying</u> all the other
       A   B   C

   places in the area, <u>I</u> couldn't find any that I liked except Lolita's.
                     D

3. <u>They were</u> <u>discovering</u> that their daughter <u>had</u> a talent for tennis,
        A   B   C

   <u>they enrolled her in a special program</u>.
                  D

4. <u>Having</u> had a bite of the baked potato, Don told <u>to his roommate</u> that <u>it</u> <u>needed</u> to be
     A   B   C   D

   cooked a little more.

5. She wishes someone <u>told</u> <u>her</u> about his <u>being</u> unemployed before <u>she</u> met him.
                               A   B   C   D

6. <u>Having turned</u> left where they <u>should turn</u> right, <u>Molly and Leo</u> had no idea where
        A   B   C

    <u>they were</u>.
       D

7. He told <u>me</u> he <u>will</u> do it the next day<u>, so</u> I don't understand why <u>he didn't.</u>
            A   B   C   D

8. She <u>didn't have to say</u> <u>that</u> because she hurt his feelings; I <u>hope</u> she <u>apologizes.</u>
                   A   B   C   D

9. I <u>was told</u> <u>that I</u> <u>bring</u> this paper to <u>this</u> office.
       A   B   C   D

10. Both jobs <u>I have been offered</u> <u>are</u> so good that I wish I <u>knew</u> for sure <u>to take.</u>
                A   B   C   D

LIVE AND LEARN

Articles

1 Complete the sentences with the correct words in parentheses.

1. _____ is everyone's responsibility. (Education, The education)

2. Will somebody please go to _____? (a blackboard, the blackboard)

3. Is there _____ ? (an extra piece of chalk, the extra piece of chalk)

4. He's a man of _____ . (honesty, the honesty)

5. Boxer High School has _____ . (a good reputation, the good reputation)

6. _____ is only skin deep. (Beauty, The beauty)

7. _____ is as important as _____ . (Common sense, The common sense) (intelligence, the intelligence)

8. _____ live longer than _____ . (Women, The women) (men, the men)

9. Here's _____ you might like to read. (an interesting article, the interesting article)

10. _____ is a necessary evil. (Money, The money)

11. Mrs. Hopkinton went to visit her husband, who's _____ for robbery. (in jail, in the jail)

12. The police are _____ at a meeting with some students. (in school, in the school)

13. What's that _____ ? (in bed, in the bed)

14. Charlie's still _____ . (in bed, in the bed)

15. Our school has _____ . (mice, the mice)

2 Fill in the blanks with *a, an,* or *the*. Leave the blank empty if no article is necessary.

A: What was _____ elementary school that you went to like?
              1

B: It was _____ old building with _____ huge yard surrounding it. In each classroom there
           2   **3**
were _____ rows of _____ brown desks. _____ desks were nailed to _____ floor;
       4   **5**   **6**   **7**
_____ seats were attached to _____ desks and were uncomfortable. Each student kept
   8   **9**
_____ cigar box in his or her desk. _____ cigar boxes were easy to find in those days,
   10   **11**
and all kids used to keep _____ crayons, _____ pair of scissors, and _____ ruler in
                 12   **13**   **14**
them. _____ teacher had _____ big desk at _____ front of _____ room. Every morning
      15   **16**   **17**   **18**
when we entered _____ classroom, we went straight to _____ cloakroom, _____ small
             19   **20**   **21**
room where we left our coats and hats. Of course, in the winter we had _____ boots, too.
                                                  22

A: What else do you remember?

B: We started class every day by singing _____ national anthem and by saying _____
                        23   **24**
Pledge of Allegiance. It's amazing that after all these years I still remember _____ words:
                                                25
I pledge allegiance to _____ flag of _____ United States of America
                          26   **27**
And to the Republic for which it stands, one nation under God indivisible
With _____ liberty and _____ justice for all.
      28   **29**

A: Do _____ schoolchildren still recite that nowadays?
      30

B: Probably. The only other thing I remember is that we had _____ break every morning
                                         31
sometime around 10:00. If _____ weather was nice, we played _____ games in _____
                    32   **33**   **34**
yard. Otherwise, we went to _____ school gym.
                         35

Verb patterns – *make/let*

3 What kind of teacher would you be? Complete the sentences with *make students* or *be made* and the correct form of the verbs in parentheses. Add *not* where necessary.

1. If I were a teacher, I would _____ (do) homework.

2. If I were a teacher, students would _____ (come) to class on time.

3. If I were a teacher, students would _____ (help) clean the school.

4. If I were a teacher, I would _____ (raise) their hand before speaking.

5. If I were a teacher, I would _____ (sit) in assigned seats.

6. If I were a teacher, students would _____ (stand up) when answering questions.

7. If I were a teacher, I would _____ (take) tests.

8. If I were a teacher, students who misbehaved would _____ (stay) after school.

4 Complete the sentences with *let students* and the correct form of the verbs in parentheses. Add *not* where necessary.

1. If I were a teacher, I would _____ (call) me by my first name.

2. If I were a teacher, I would _____ (eat) in class.

3. If I were a teacher, I would _____ (throw) paper airplanes around the classroom.

4. If I were a teacher, I would _____ (take) long breaks.

5. If I were a teacher, I would _____ (leave) the room without permission.

6. If I were a teacher, I would _____ (tell) me how to teach.

Verb patterns – subjunctive

5 Rewrite the sentences with a *that*-clause.

1. The teacher asked the student to come with her parents.

    The teacher asked that the student come with her parents _____.

2. "Mr. Norberg, tell me why you didn't give my daughter a good recommendation?" the student's father demanded.

    _____

    _____.

3. It is important for you to be available for college interviews.

    _____.

4. We suggest his applying to at least three colleges.

    _____.

5. "Ellen, could you please help me with my application?" I requested.

    _____.

6. It is necessary for the college to know your qualifications.

   _____ .

7. I recommend her visiting the colleges she's interested in attending.

   _____ .

8. It was essential for them to get their applications in on time.

   _____ .

9. They advised me to talk to a counselor about which colleges to apply to.

   _____ .

10. "You must talk to your teacher about the problem," my mother insisted.

    _____ .

Verb patterns – verbs of perception

6 Complete the sentences with the base form or the present participle of the verbs in parentheses.

1. I heard someone _____ (walk) around in the dark.

2. I heard two people _____ (talk).

3. Then I thought I heard someone _____ (scream), but it happened so quickly that I couldn't be sure.

4. I was so scared that I could feel my whole body _____ (shake).

5. I saw a stranger _____ (pick up) what looked like a weapon.

6. Then I saw the stranger and another person _____ (enter) the house; a few seconds later the light went on.

7. A few minutes later, I saw one of the people _____ (carry) a TV out of the building, when suddenly a police car turned around the corner.

8. I watched the stranger _____ (drop) the TV when he saw the police.

9. I watched the stranger _____ (empty) his pockets.

10. I watched the police _____ (take) the man to the police car, but I never actually saw him _____ (get) in because just at that moment the phone rang.

Stems and affixes

7 The words in the boxes contain the same stems. Match the stems in Row A with their meanings in Row B.

| import
export
deport | cap
capital
captain | motion
motor
promote | audience
auditorium
audiovisual | vacant
vacation
vacuum | evidence
video
vision |

A	1. audi	2. cap	3. mot	4. port	5. vac	6. vid, vis
B	a. empty	b. carry	c. see	d. head	e. move	f. hear

8 Use your knowledge of the meaning of the stems in Exercise 7 to complete each sentence with a word from the box.

| audible   decapitate   demote   evacuate   invisible   porter |

1. If you leave a building during an emergency, you _____ it.

2. Something you can hear is_____ .

3. Someone who carries your bags to your hotel room is a _____.

4. To cut off the head of an animal, for example, is to _____ the animal.

5. Something that can't be seen is _____ .

6. To change a person's job from manager to assistant manager is to _____ the person.

Vocabulary check

9 Each sentence has an underlined word or phrase. Below each sentence are four other words or phrases marked (A), (B), (C), and (D). You are to choose the <u>one</u> word or phrase that <u>best keeps the meaning</u> of the original sentence if it is substituted for the underlined word or phrase. Circle the correct answer.

1. The residents of the town <u>thoroughly searched</u> the area in search of the missing child.
   A. accomplished
   B. assigned
   C. combed
   D. dreaded

2. It wasn't easy for them to <u>achieve</u> what they had set out to do, but in the end they succeeded.
   A. accomplish
   B. assign
   C. comb
   D. dread

3. Hot, humid weather is not <u>favorable</u> to working outdoors.
   A. arbitrary
   B. conducive
   C. consistent
   D. daunting

4. It will be a <u>very difficult</u> task for the government to convince voters that higher taxes are necessary.
   A. arbitrary
   B. conducive
   C. consistent
   D. daunting

5. Her schoolwork is <u>constantly</u> of poor quality.
   A. arbitrarily
   B. conducively
   C. consistently
   D. dauntingly

6. The children who were allowed to join the team were chosen <u>seemingly without reason</u>.
   A. arbitrarily
   B. conducively
   C. consistently
   D. dauntingly

7. You must realize that we face several <u>limitations</u>.
   A. challenges
   B. constraints
   C. contradictions
   D. consultants

8. <u>Not giving up on your hard work</u> will pay off.
   A. Challenge
   B. Dread
   C. Frustration
   D. Perseverance

9. Running the 1,000-meter race was a great <u>difficulty</u> for the blind runner, so he was very happy when he finished in second place.
   A. challenge
   B. constraint
   C. contradiction
   D. dread

10. Older people sometimes have <u>great fear and anxiety</u> of being alone.
    A. a great challenge
    B. a great constraint
    C. a great contradiction
    D. a great dread

Structure and written expression

10 **Each sentence has four underlined words or phrases. The four underlined parts of the sentence are marked (A), (B), (C), and (D). Identify the <u>one</u> underlined word or phrase that must be changed in order for the sentence to be grammatically correct. Circle the appropriate letter.**

1. We suggest that she <u>sees</u> <u>the</u> psychiatrist our son <u>has been going</u> <u>to</u>.
                     A   B   C   D

2. <u>The</u> generosity is <u>a</u> characteristic <u>to</u> praise and <u>to honor</u>.
     A   B   C   D

3. <u>The</u> area that you are referring <u>to</u> and <u>under observation</u> is <u>being</u> put up for sale.
     A   B   C   D

4. <u>The</u> director made <u>the</u> consultant <u>to do</u> the report again<u>, so</u> she was not very pleased.
     A   B   C   D

5. To have <u>patience</u> and <u>being</u> understanding are <u>the</u> qualities <u>a teacher most needs</u>.
           A   B   C   D

6. <u>The</u> high school principal demanded that the teacher <u>be</u> in the main office
     A   B

   immediately after <u>finish</u> <u>the</u> last class of the day.
                          C   D

7. <u>Looking out</u> the window, I could see someone <u>stand</u> behind <u>a tree</u> across <u>the street</u>.
     A   B   C   D

8. Before <u>being allowed to take</u> <u>the</u> elevator, I was made <u>sign</u> my name at <u>the</u> reception desk.
               A   B   C   D

9. We didn't let <u>her go</u> because <u>of the rain</u> and <u>because</u> we needed <u>the</u> car.
              A   B   C   D

10. Unlike when I was <u>in school</u>, it is very common nowadays to see <u>children</u> <u>doing</u>
                     A   B   C

    schoolwork on <u>the</u> computers.
                   D

ANSWER KEY

VOLUME A

Unit One

1 1. No 2. Yes 3. Maybe 4. No 5. No 6. Maybe
7. Maybe

2 2. There wouldn't be many homeless people if
they could find jobs. 3. There would be jobs if the
economy weren't bad. 4. If the economy improves
soon, more people will be able to find jobs. 5. If
people donate money, they will help the homeless
find somewhere to live. 6. If the government
builds cheap housing, homeless people will stop
living on the street. 7. If the government had
enough money to provide low-income housing, it
would do something. 8. If the government weren't
afraid to raise taxes, it would have enough money.
9. The situation may change if there's an election
soon. 10. The government will be able to do
something about the homeless situation if a new
leader raises taxes.

3 1. even if 2. In case 3. unless 4. provided
that

4 2. What would you do with it if you were me?
3. Of course, I would buy you something with the
money if you needed something. 4. I would break
up with him if I weren't afraid of not being able to
meet anyone else. 5. I know that's a stupid reason
to stay with someone, but I bet you would do the
same if you were me.

5 2. He wishes he didn't live far from his brother.
3. He wishes he had somebody his own age to talk
to. 4. He wishes he didn't have serious problems
with his health. 5. He wishes he didn't have to
spend a lot of money on medicine. 6. He wishes
his children would do their own laundry. 7. He
wishes they helped more around the house.
8. He wishes his son didn't/wouldn't stay out all
night. 9. He wishes his daughter would get
married. 10. He wishes his daughter would try
to find a boyfriend. 11. He wishes both of his
children would move out of his home and find
places of their own.

6 1. up 2. off 3. down on 4. in 5. out 6. up
with 7. up 8. to 9. out

7 1. D 2. B 3. D 4. A 5. C 6. B 7. C 8. A
9. C 10. D

8 1. D 2. A 3. C 4. B 5. C 6. B 7. D 8. C
9. C 10. B

Unit Two

1 2. who suffer from abnormal worry and anxiety –
subject 3. that the psychiatrist prescribes for them –
object 4. which they take – object 5. that the
psychiatrist will not give medication to – object
6. that will help the people understand their
problem – subject 7. that he or she asks – object
8. who asks a lot of personal questions – subject. In
3, 4, 5 and 7, the relative pronouns are unnecessary.

2 2. whose class he is in 3. you need to get off at
4. I eat 5. whose paintings are in that part of
the museum 6. who/that live near the border
7. I tried on 8. I wasn't expecting 9. who/that kept
kicking each other 10. whose votes they want

3 1. grandparents 2. remark 3. story 4. building
5. thought 6. money 7. conversation 8. flowers
9. face 10. fear

4 1. tiring 2. boring 3. confused 4. shocking
5. relaxing 6. interested 7. amusing 8. amazed
9. depressing 10. excited

5 2. He might be. 3. It might have. 4. They might.
5. He might be. 6. He might have. 7. She might.
8. I might have.

6 2. It's possible they have already left. 3. It's
possible he will faint. 4. It's possible she's talking
on the phone. 5. It's possible he didn't hear you.
6. It wasn't possible for them to write/to have
written that. 7. It was possible for her to stay later,
but she didn't want to. 8. It's possible he
won't/doesn't like it. 9. It's possible they didn't
have time. 10. It wasn't possible for her to make/to
have made such a beautiful cake.

7 2. She may/might not have the time. 3. They
may/might get lost. 4. They may/might be
training for a race. 5. She may/might be visiting
her mother. 6. He may/might be fixing the car.

8 2. I couldn't have left the keys in the car. 3. He
may/might not have known where to go. 4. She
may/might have gone swimming. 5. They could
have gone abroad, but they didn't want to. 6. They
may/might not have gotten to the airport on time.

9 1. B 2. C 3. B 4. D 5. D 6. C 7. C 8. B
9. D 10. A

10 1. D 2. A 3. D 4. C 5. B 6. D 7. D 8. C
9. A 10. B

Unit Three

1 1. was babysitting 2. were working 3. didn't like
4. was talking 5. lasted 6. paid 7. was sleeping
8. decided 9. was getting dressed 10. was eating

2 1. were you doing; Were you fixing; Did you fix
2. Did you see; was she wearing 3. was fighting;
were they fighting; Did the teacher try; broke up
4. was she talking; were they talking; Did/Didn't
you ask

3 1. has arrived; arrived; began; has reported 2. has
broken out; have arrived; haven't completely put
out; has begun; started 3. was; died; have not
released; has been able to

4 2. Gary has been retired since 1991/for … years.
3. Linda has been working/has worked at the
University of Arizona since 1993/for … years.
4. Gary has been looking for a part-time job since
1993/for … years. 5. He's been waiting to hear
about the job for two days. 6. Linda and Gary have
had a used car since they moved to Arizona/for …
years. 7. Linda and Gary have taken many
photographs of the beautiful landscape of Arizona.
8. Linda and Gary have been to the Grand Canyon.
9. Gary has been painting their house since last
week/for one week. 10. Linda and Gary have made
many new friends.

5 1. C 2. D 3. B 4. A 5. D 6. D 7. D 8. B
9. C 10. A

6 1. A 2. C 3. C 4. B 5. D 6. D 7. C 8. B
9. C 10. C

Unit Four

1 1. had finished the test; yes 2. hadn't driven;
no; A 3. the meeting had started; no; A 4. had
gone to the same school; no; A 5. had escaped; yes
6. had been President; no; A

2 2. had left their fingerprints all over the victim's
car. 3. had been driving the same route to work for
years. 4. had been sitting in a red Chevrolet all
night long before the day of the kidnapping.
5. hadn't called in three days. 6. had destroyed the
car in an accident. 7. had been driving 95 miles per
hour. 8. had been eating/had eaten only stale bread
and potato chips for four days. 9. had bought
airplane tickets. 10. had been fighting.

3 1. haven't written 2. took 3. have been trying
4. have been thinking 5. haven't made up 6. had
thought/had been thinking 7. had even applied
8. met 9. happened 10. saw 11. was going

12. was coming 13. had been studying 14. hadn't
seen 15. didn't recognize 16. has/had lost
17. has/had been 18. heard 19. was starting/had
started 20. had happened 21. were 22. have I
been looking 23. haven't found 24. have been
working 25. called 26. has gotten 27. had been
looking 28. found

4 1. a) past b) past c) yes d) no 2. a) past
b) present c) no d) no 3. a) present b) present
c) yes d) yes 4. a) past b) present c) yes d) no
5. a) past b) past c) no d) yes

5 (Possible answers)
2. If my mother hadn't married my father, she
would have married another man. 3. I wouldn't be
close to my cousins if we hadn't spent a lot of time
together when we were children. 4. If we hadn't
grown up in a big house, we wouldn't all have had
our own bedrooms. 5. I wouldn't have had to share
things with my brother and sister if my parents had
bought us a lot. 6. My mother would have had to
work if my father hadn't had a very good job. 7. If
my brother had liked school, he wouldn't have
dropped out and joined the army. 8. If my sister
hadn't moved far away a few years ago, we would
see her often.

6 2. Had my mother not married my father, she
would have married another man. 3. I wouldn't be
close to my cousins had we not spent a lot of time
together when we were children. 4. Had we not
grown up in a big house, we wouldn't all have had
our own bedrooms. 5. I wouldn't have had to share
things with my brother and sister had my parents
bought us a lot. 6. My mother would have had to
work had my father not had a very good job.
7. Had my brother liked school, he wouldn't have
dropped out and joined the army. 8. Had my sister
not moved far away a few years ago, we would see
her often.

7 1. would have picked; had told 2. would have;
had passed 3. had; would be 4. would never have
met; hadn't decided 5. miss; will have to 6. had
had; would be 7. wouldn't have bought; had
known 8. would help; knew 9. doesn't come; will
be 10. would spend; had invented 11. would have
come 12. would have gone 13. would call
14. would have sent 15. would take

8 1. B 2. A 3. C 4. A 5. C 6. B 7. D 8. C
9. D 10. A

9 1. B 2. D 3. D 4. D 5. D 6. A 7. D 8. B
9. D 10. C

Unit Five

1 X - 1, 3, 4, 5, 8

2 1. was needed   2. was destroyed   3. is being bought/She is buying some ice cream.   4. was named; was killed   5. would have been visited/If Natalie's relatives and friends had known she was in the hospital, they would have visited her.   6. was heard/I was afraid because the noise that I heard was so loud.   7. to be identified   8. has been turned down   9. may have been hit/The blue car may have hit the white car.   10. was seen/The woman was walking down the street when she saw a bag full of money; she didn't know what to do with it.

3 1. broke out   2. was destroyed   3. has been estimated   4. were injured   5. (were) taken   6. was treated   7. has been put out   8. is being investigated   9. has learned   10. was seen   11. were found   12. have/has found out   13. had been dismissed   14. has not been released   15. has been picked up   16. is being questioned   17. is expected

4 2. you should have someone take care of it.   3. she had it made.   4. he's having it changed.   5. he has had someone type them.   6. I would have gotten the police to take her to the hospital.   7. they're going to get a photographer to take them.   8. I would get a caterer to prepare it.   9. I got it shoveled.   10. I'm going to get it translated.

5 2. I have to get this jacket dry-cleaned.   3. The blind woman has someone drive her to work.   4. I have had the car looked at three times.   5. Are you going to get someone to remodel your kitchen?   6. You need to get your hair cut.   7. Did you get someone to pick you up?   8. We are going to get the store to deliver the air-conditioner.

6 1. D   2. C   3. D   4. B   5. A   6. B   7. D   8. D   9. A   10. C

7 1. C   2. C   3. D   4. A   5. B   6. C   7. C   8. D   9. D   10. D

Unit Six

1 2. going out – object of a verb   3. living – object of a preposition   4. Making – subject   5. marrying – object of a preposition   6. Being exposed – subject   7. sharing – object of a preposition

2 2. for being late.   3. for breaking the machine.   4. of waiting.   5. of becoming an astronaut.   6. about standing in line.   7. in applying for the supervisor's job.   8. on getting the scholarship.

9. for (their) not getting the loan.   10. on learning all the verb forms.

3 2. Going on the picnic could have been fun.   3. Appointing him treasurer of the organization was foolish.   4. Going by train will take us less time than going by bus.   5. In that city, seeing beggars on the street is unusual.   6. Not studying the language before we moved to the country was a mistake.   7. Running your own business can require very long hours.   8. Being the only female on the team would be impossible.   9. Being a participant in this group has been a good experience for me.   10. Feeling loved is very important for children.

4 2. has quit smoking.   3. intends to drive to the picnic.   4. doesn't recall seeing the suspect in front of the house.   5. promises not to be late.   6. avoided talking to her brother about the money.   7. misses eating her mother's cooking.   8. has decided to go to Brazil for two weeks.   9. keeps trying to lose weight.   10. refuses to help Mimi with her homework.

5 1. used to work   2. didn't use to make   3. am used to working   4. wasn't used to doing   5. used to kill   6. weren't used to having   7. used to be able   8. are used to being   9. am used to lifting   10. used to be

6 1. Discrimination   2. oblige   3. endorsement   4. resignation   5. equal   6. involvement   7. responsibility   8. aspire   9. Exclusion   10. discourage

7 1. D   2. C   3. C   4. D   5. B   6. B   7. D   8. B   9. A   10. C

8 1. B   2. A   3. B   4. A   5. C   6. C   7. B   8. C   9. B   10. D

VOLUME B

Unit One

1 2. which 3. whose 4. who 5. whose 6. who
7. who 8. which 9. which 10. which 11. who

2 1. Many things that are taken for granted today
did not catch on when they were first created.
4. That's why the inventors that are showing their
latest creations at this year's annual Unknown
Inventors Conference are confident that one day
their inventions will be useful. 7. She told me that
acquaintances and relatives that have seen her
invention often say, "Gee, Bea, it's nice, but …"
10. As far as I'm concerned, an automatic table-setter
is nice, but setting the table is not a household task
that is terribly time-consuming or boring. 11. To all
you inventors that are listening to me, would one of
you invent a machine that does all my ironing?

3 (line 3) , which is the year my great-grandfather
was born, (line 5) who had very strange ideas
(line 7) , which is the descendant of your steam
motorcycle. (line 8) that you needed to open a
factory (line 9) , whose name is usually associated
with the automobile, (line 10) which are on the
road today (line 13) , which comes from
petroleum, (line 14) , who controls the direction of
his or her car by holding a steering wheel, (line 15) ,
where the driver sits on the right. (line 17) , which
have replaced what was woodland in your day.
(line 19) which are designed to allow speed limits of
up to 65 miles per hour. (line 21) , which is
necessary if drivers are to be able to get out of their
cars to go to work or to do their shopping. (line 22)
who park in these parking lots (line 24) which the
descendant of your steam motorcycle has caused
(line 26) whom you talked to about your steam
motorcycle (line 27) who started society on this
revolutionary path.

4 1. It's funny that you should have had so much
trouble raising the money you needed to open a
factory since Henry Ford, whose name is usually
associated with the automobile, made a fortune.
2. I could go on describing the changes the
descendant of your steam motorcycle has caused
but, hopefully, this short letter gives you a fairly
good idea. 3. It is a shame that most people you
talked to about your steam motorcycle paid so little
attention to your idea.

5 2. non-defining 3. non-defining 4. non-defining
5. defining 6. non-defining 7. non-defining
8. defining

6 1. Last night I went to a concert that/which was
held at Theater Hall. 2. Theater Hall, which seats up
to 5,000 people, was packed. 3. The concert starred
Sid and Rich Mariani, who are two brothers with a
well-known radio program. 4. The radio program,
which is called *Talk of the House*, is on 88.7 FM every
Monday evening at 8:00. 5. I'm sure that most, if
not all, of the people who/that attended the concert
are devoted listeners of this very funny program.
6. During the program, people call the radio station
to talk to the two brothers, who answer the callers'
questions about how to fix things around the house.
7. The callers, who can be as funny as Sid and Rich,
sometimes ask the strangest questions. 8. If you are
someone who/that has never listened to the
program, you should tune in next Monday at 8:00.

7 2. It is hard to believe that people in those days
thought that you were a man who had very strange
ideas because nowadays most of us can't imagine
existence without our automobile, the descendant
of your steam motorcycle. 3. In fact, many cars on
the road today are called Fords. 4. This is a great
shame, but people these days are often in a hurry,
so they need to use roads designed to allow speed
limits of up to 65 miles per hour.

8 2. July 4th, which is Independence Day, is a
national holiday. 3. The students who/that are
standing outside the classroom are there because
they are late. 4. The movie which/that is being
filmed near the waterfront is due to come out next
year. 5. The people who/that are living in that
building will have to be evacuated. 6. Our youngest
child, who was born in Alaska, has always wanted to
move back there. 7. Students who/that were taking
the test in Bulger Hall yesterday complained that
they smelled smoke even before the fire alarm went
off. 8. Her latest book, which was published just
three months ago, is already a huge success.

9 (Possible answers)
2. the inventor of the telephone. 3. cooked in butter.
4. played indoors. 5. in the bathroom. 6. protesting
in front of City Hall.

10 1. C 2. B 3. D 4. C 5. A 6. A 7. C 8. D
9. A 10. B

11 1. A 2. A 3. C 4. C 5. D 6. D 7. A 8. D
9. C 10. C

Unit Two

1 1. should be; should have taken off 2. should be eating 3. should be getting 4. should have arrived 5. should be calling 6. should have had; should be having 7. should have met 8. should have

2 2. should 3. might/could 4. might/could 5. might/could 6. could not 7. should 8. might/could 9. should 10. should 11. might not 12. should not 13. might/could 14. might/could 15. should

3 1. a) No; No b) Yes; Yes 2. a) Yes; No b) Yes; Yes/Probably 3. a) Yes; No b) No; Yes 4. a) No; Yes b) Yes; Probably 5. a) No; No b) Yes; No c) Yes; Yes

4 2. 'll be working. 3. 'll be studying. 4. 'll be waiting for Anna 5. 'll be painting the house. 6. 'll be fixing breakfast. 7. 'll be talking to Tony. 8. 'll be traveling to China.

5 2. In two months, I'll have saved $500. 3. Philip will have left by 8:30. 4. The soccer game will have ended by 4:00. 5. The food will have been served by noon. 6. The children will have gotten on the bus by 7:30. 7. The car will have been fixed by tomorrow afternoon. 8. The trash will have been picked up by 10:00. 9. She'll have gotten up when you call. 10. The pictures will have been developed by tomorrow.

6 1. starving 2. tiny 3. boiling 4. gigantic 5. filthy 6. freezing 7. exhausted 8. spotless 9. furious 10. hilarious

7 1. B 2. C 3. B 4. C 5. A 6. C 7. D 8. A 9. A 10. B

8 1. B 2. D 3. C 4. A 5. D 6. D 7. D 8. B 9. A 10. C

Unit Three

1 2. We had hoped to change our seats. A number of seats were empty. 3. The players did not seem to be playing their best. Both of the players make a lot of money. 4. The fans were not pleased. The majority of the fans had paid a lot of money for their seats. 5. Nat Tedesco seemed to be less affected by the hot, humid weather. All of Nat Tedesco's training was in Puerto Rico. 6. During the match, my mother-in-law kept asking about the rules of the game. She couldn't understand a few of the rules at all. 7. The fans were also not happy with the referee. They thought some of the referee's calls were unfair. 8. At the end of the match we

bought some souvenirs. Two of the souvenirs were for my husband.

2 2. Cindy Norton and Martha Frankel, both of whom own a successful clothing store, spoke to us about the difficulties they faced when they first started up. 3. They needed to raise a lot of money, most of which they were able to get from two banks. 4. Before they found the right location for their store, they had looked at many places, most of which were either too expensive or too small. 5. The women, neither of whose families is involved in the business, have very little time for themselves. 6. A lack of time for themselves is common to all these businesspeople, several of whom we talked to about this problem. 7. Finding the right workers is also a problem for our store owners, the majority of whom have at least ten employees. 8. We wondered if these businesspeople's employees, very few of whose names we managed to get, were treated better than the businesspeople themselves had been treated when they were working for someone else. 9. Other information, much of which we found surprising, is included in our article, "Are you tired of it all?"

3 3. Before my mother sent us off to school in the morning, she used to make us a big breakfast. 4. Before my children go to school, they make their own breakfast. 5. While I did my homework, I was never allowed to listen to the radio. 6. While Stephen and Rachel do their homework, they sit in front of the television. 7. After we got home from school, we would always find my mother's cookies and some milk on the table. 8. After our kids get out of school, they go to a fast-food place with their friends. 9. When my children enter our empty house at the end of the school day, they know to lock the door right away and not let in any strangers. 10. When my mother met us at the front door of our home at the end of the school day, she always greeted each of us with a big hug and kiss. 11. Since I've had children of my own, I realize how much our way of life has changed.

4 2. While going up on the elevator, she started talking to a colleague about a problem. 3. When getting her files, she saw her boss. 4. After talking to her boss for half an hour, she knew she had more work to do at home tonight. 5. Since getting the new job, she has very little free time. 6. She went to the supermarket before going home. 7. After going home, she put a frozen dinner in the microwave oven. 8. While eating dinner, she talked on the phone. 9. After hanging up, she sent a fax. 10. While sending a fax, she answered the phone again. 11. She wrote two memos before going to bed. 12. Since moving into her new home, she hasn't had any time to enjoy it.

5 3. obligation 4. lack of obligation 5. logical deduction 6. unfulfilled possibility 7. obligation 8. possibility 9. logical deduction 10. possibility 11. impossibility 12. unfulfilled expectation 13. logical deduction 14. expectation

6 2. They must have made a mistake. 3. We didn't have to pay 4. Other customers must be calling 5. I had to wait 6. You must have been thinking 7. I didn't have to wait 8. They must not have been 9. You must not have called 10. There must have been 11. We have to/must cut down 12. He must be bringing

7 1. Resumption 2. qualification 3. participate 4. consume 5. realization 6. notification 7. assume 8. presumption 9. generalize 10. memorization

8 1. B 2. C 3. B 4. D 5. D 6. A 7. C 8. C 9. A 10. A

9 1. A 2. B 3. A 4. D 5. A 6. C 7. C 8. D 9. C 10. C

Unit Four

1 1. shouldn't let 2. should I do 3. ought to tell 4. ought to cheat 5. ought to say 6. ought to help 7. should I do 8. Should I say 9. ought to mind your own business 10. shouldn't get involved 11. ought to get up the nerve 12. ought to encourage 13. ought to check

2 1. shouldn't 2. shouldn't 3. should 4. have to 5. shouldn't 6. doesn't have to 7. don't have to 8. have to 9. shouldn't 10. should

3 2. I saw someone enter only once while I was sitting in the waiting room. 3. People fully understand what it is like only when they find themselves in a similar situation. 4. I will go only if you go. 5. Each police officer paid a $50,000 fine, and went to jail for one year. 6. The region has not been hit by such bad weather conditions since 1973. 7. I would not think them for one moment capable of such an awful crime. 8. People can no longer throw things away without thinking about the consequences.

4 2. c Never again will you pay higher taxes. 3. e In no case should you leave your baggage unattended. 4. d Under no circumstances should this be put in water. 5. f Rarely is it necessary to operate. 6. b Nowhere in the world could I have met someone else like you. 7. g Never again do I want to see you do that.

5 2. what time it was 3. what it was 4. where the smell was coming from 5. that it was coming from there 6. who he was 7. how we were able to sleep/could sleep/could have slept/had been able to sleep 8. what the problem was 9. where the smell was coming from 10. how much it had cost

6 2. How many dinosaurs inhabited the earth 3. How big the dinosaur was 4. How often scientists find dinosaur fossils 5. Whether people will ever know for sure how the dinosaur died out 6. How scientists found the first dinosaur fossils 7. Whether it is important for scientists to learn more about dinosaurs 8. Whether the Natural History Museum has displayed all the dinosaur bones in its collection 9. Which museum has the biggest collection of dinosaur fossils 10. Why the movies about dinosaurs are so popular

7 (Possible answers)
2. Who is going on the ship is being kept a secret. 3. Why the ship is making this particular voyage is also not being made public. 4. How long the journey will take hasn't been decided yet. 5. What the environmental group did during their last protest upset government officials. 6. Where the organization's headquarters is located is well-known.

8 1. A 2. D 3. C 4. A 5. C 6. C 7. A 8. B 9. D 10. C

9 1. A 2. C 3. D 4. D 5. B 6. B 7. A 8. B 9. B 10. D

Unit Five

1 (Possible answers)
2. it was free. 3. if I was from Miami. 4. I was from Canada. 5. I was visiting college friends and taking a break from the cold. 6. where I was from in Canada. 7. I was from Quebec. 8. if I speak/spoke French. 9. I did. 10. if he did too. 11. he spoke a little. 12. he had studied it for two years in college. 13. I had been in Florida. 14. I had been in Orlando for four days and I had been in Miami 15. how long I was staying. 16. I would be in the Miami area for another week or so. 17. I was free, maybe we could meet one night for dinner or for a drink. 18. I didn't know 19. I would have to ask my husband.

2 2. passenger 3. passenger. 4. flight attendant 5. passenger 6. flight attendant 7. passenger 8. flight attendant 9. flight attendant 10. passenger

3 2. The passenger asked the flight attendant to give his wife a glass of water. 3. The passenger asked the flight attendant to bring her husband a blanket. 4. The flight attendant told us not to smoke until the captain turned off the 'no smoking' sign. 5. The passenger asked the flight attendant to tell him/her where their seats were. 6. The flight attendant told everyone to stay seated until the plane came to a complete stop. 7. The passenger asked the flight attendant to tell him/her what the movie was. 8. The flight attendant told the passengers not to use any electronic devices during takeoff and landing. 9. The flight attendant told the passengers to fasten their seat belts. 10. The passenger asked the flight attendant to help his wife and him fill in the customs form.

4 1. should have kept; shouldn't have said; should call; should I say 2. shouldn't have worn; should have worn; should have listened 3. should we serve; should serve; should have thought 4. shouldn't eat; shouldn't have bought; should have come; shouldn't enjoy

5 2. You should take out our tickets now. 3. They might/may be in my bag. 4. You might/may have put them there by mistake. 5. I couldn't have put them there. 6. I must have put them in the brown suitcase. 7. you shouldn't have checked it. 8. You didn't have to check it. 9. We could have taken it on the plane with us. 10. You should have told me that before I checked it. 11. We have to explain what has happened. 12. we should say. 13. They must be looking for us. 14. All the other passengers must have already boarded the plane. 15. You shouldn't have talked to me like that. 16. I should have stayed home.

6 1. present 2. past 3. past 4. past 5. past 6. present 7. past 8. present 9. past 10. present

7 2. the hotel room had had a TV. 3. she had taken a/the plane. 4. she hadn't paid for the hotel in advance. 5. she hadn't gone to the island with her cousin. 6. it hadn't rained most of the time she was on the island. 7. she had taken warm enough clothing for the cool weather. 8. her pictures had come out. 9. her boyfriend had gone with her. 10. she had mailed the post cards from the post office/she hadn't mailed the postcards from the hotel.

8 1. D 2. B 3. C 4. B 5. D 6. B 7. A 8. D 9. C 10. A

9 1. D 2. C 3. A 4. B 5. A 6. B 7. B 8. A 9. B 10. D

Unit Six

1 1. Education 2. the blackboard 3. an extra piece of chalk 4. honesty 5. a good reputation 6. Beauty 7. Common sense, intelligence 8. Women, men

9. an interesting article 10. Money 11. in jail 12. in the school 13. in the bed 14. in bed 15. mice

2 1. the 2. an 3. a 4. – 5. – 6. The 7. the 8. the 9. the 10. a 11. – 12. – 13. a 14. a 15. The 16. a 17. the 18. the 19. the 20. the 21. a 22. – 23. the 24. the 25. the 26. the 27. the 28. – 29. – 30. – 31. a 32. the 33. – 34. the 35. the

3 1. make students do/not make students do 2. be made to come/not be made to come 3. be made to help/not be made to help 4. make students raise/not make students raise 5. make students sit/not make students sit 6. be made to stand up/not be made to stand up 7. make students take/not make students take 8. be made to stay/not be made to stay

4 1. let students call/not let students call 2. let students eat/not let students eat 3. let students throw/not let students throw 4. let students take/not let students take 5. let students leave/not let students leave 6. let students tell/not let students tell

5 2. The student's father demanded that Mr. Norberg tell him why he didn't give/hadn't given his daughter a good recommendation. 3. It is important that you be available for college interviews. 4. We suggest that he apply to at least three colleges. 5. I requested that Ellen help me with my application. 6. It is necessary that the college know your qualifications. 7. I recommend that she visit the colleges she's interested in attending. 8. It was essential that they get their applications in on time. 9. They advised that I talk to a counselor about which colleges to apply to. 10. My mother insisted that I talk to my teacher about the problem.

6 1. walking 2. talking 3. scream 4. shaking 5. pick up 6. enter 7. carrying 8. drop 9. empty/emptying 10. take/taking; get

7 1. f 2. d 3. e 4. b 5. a 6. c

8 1. evacuate 2. audible 3. porter 4. decapitate 5. invisible 6. demote

9 1. C 2. A 3. B 4. D 5. C 6. A 7. B 8. D 9. A 10. D

10 1. A 2. A 3. C 4. C 5. B 6. C 7. B 8. C 9. B 10. D